Karma Through the Window of Time

The Spiritual Journey of the 2 Angels

VIE Loriot de Rouvray

ISBN: 979-8-9897845-5-4 Paperback

ISBN: 979-8-9897845-6-1 Hardback

Printed in the United States of America

Dedication

I dedicate this book to Mother Mary "Undoer of Knots" and the Highest Flame of the Universe "BLUE FLAME"

"Reality in the grants, the realistic life of authors CHADD & VIE mesmerizing attentiveness, you must wake up."

This book is part of the series of writings by CHADD & VIE. They are lessons in expanding your mind, opening up your consciousness, and having you take a trip.

Each one of our books takes you on a journey or a trip.

Table of Contents

The Inside Out

A wounded undercover FBI agent and the catalyst of several books are on the inside of a major international scandal. There is a woman and a man named Al Kadir Kalssam, who also goes by the name of Al Kidir, involved with ISIS and Al Qaeda and the drug trade that keeps America afloat. They are involved with every psychiatric unit in town.

True or false – is this fiction or is it a fact – it is yours to find out.

This is my story. I am with the Institute of Light and Sound and work for the Messiah the King.

I never married on earth until I met VIE.

I have prayed a lot for this. I am convinced that Dave Youth, who goes as Doc Youth, is just as guilty as myself. Now who are you going to trust?

We, CHADD & VIE, "the God Duo," have infiltrated the inside of this operation called "Death of America" by the Pakistan and Iranian Governments that have sent death to America.

As Americans, we are ready to retire from the government and go into holistic and healing sessions of God's work.

Our act of righteousness is to save our children even after the negative consequences of the Tri-Regional Psychiatric and Associates on our children. A deep trance will fall upon the Al Kidir who are disciples of Satan.

I, CHADD, must do my duty as one of the Angels at work in Orange County. I need to let you know that darkness has enveloped the Al Kidir office.

The demons are pills, like Seroquel, Xanax, and Vicodin...These pills give a false feeling of relief and at the same time cause addiction in your DNA.

Your DNA is compromised at that point, and you become vulnerable spiritually. Beelzebub, Satan, and Lucifer (the devils have many names, just like God) love Aftab Al Kidir, who disguised herself because of her pill-pushing. The pills are demons pushing on our children of Orlando.

I looked at her in the eyes, and I saw this black, demonic, empty woman in the vessel of a beautiful Indian human being. It was an empty shell. And all her associates are the same. I saw them turning their eyes blue. They have no souls.

Dr. Dick Sanity, on the other side of a demonic roam, is married to Betsy, the nurse that prescribes pills for Tri-Regional and Associates.

These demons need to be eliminated from the equation.

A message from the other side: attention bon spur Betsy, you are going to hell in your next life. You'll be looked upon as a cockroach, respected as a water moccasin, and looked on as a child molester. You have no soul; you have sold it to ISIS.

I have one perfect friend I can speak with in the MBI, who is now retired. His name is Amir Zimmerman. A very high-ranking man.

Curiosity killed the cat. Some people take drugs out of curiosity. They just want to see what it is like. We forget that curiosity killed the cat. And drugs are killing thousands every year because of peer pressure.

A lot of people fall into this category regardless of race, creed, color, size, shape, or culture.

Jesus wants us to receive his life and enjoy it to the fullest naturally.

Generation X must have freedom of expression as they are born free. They are children of God. What is it all about? Keep reading; you'll find out.

From ancient times people have worshiped things and people rather than God. It goes back to the story of Adam and Eve and the serpent. The serpent tempted Adam and Eve, promising that if they ate the forbidden fruit, they would be like God.

As I am baptized, and now in the Catholic religion, the Holy Spirit dwells in my house, and therefore God is in me. And all human beings are created in the image of God but that does not mean that we are God. God is God, and we are creatures, totally dependent on God for every breath we take.

Surely, we must take hold of our destiny to build a world of love, peace, and justice! The Miracle Tone, 528 MHz, is one of the keys.

We will never achieve that without being humble before God and putting our trust in Jesus Christ our Redeemer.

Beware of false prophets such as Kenny Yon and be very wary of those pushing psychotropic drugs, such as Tri-Regional Psychiatric Center and the ones across the Dolphin Land.

As parishioners, we would dearly love to see the Asylums for the Indigent and the Other Asylums in Baker or Entrapment County shut down. Because active human slavery exists in this melting pot on planet Earth.

Introduction

VIE and I were on the I-75 and blew a tire of our Cayenne. We called for assistance with the flat tire. It was very hot that day, over one hundred F, and we waited for a very long time. Then suddenly a white van showed up with tinted windows to repair the tire.

As it was hot, they offered us a drink, but that was a ruse. Then they drugged us both and kidnapped us.

We woke up in an asylum at the Florida-Georgia border.

As we were taken away, the driver of the van asked me if I knew of a man named Doctor Youth with his church, and I replied, "Yes, I know Youth." Edward Cayce was sitting next to the driver.

They took us on a four-hour journey. We were gagged in the back of the van but comfortable. Then they proceeded to give VIE and me a raw hypno and continued to drive us into an undisclosed Christian camp.

When we woke up, twelve hours had passed, and we were inside a cell.

Pierre Montour de la Roux found a way to approach us alone in our cell, to talk to us. He introduced himself to let us know that he had been in vibrational communication with Commandant Sheran and knew what was going to happen to us.

Suddenly, a strong wind blew inside the cell and two Gladiators—that's what they looked like— entered by the door and left the passage to Commandant Sheran. Without a word, Commandant Sheran clicked his fingers, and we found ourselves tele-transported into his spacecraft.

We were inside an enormous military aircraft designed to fly in any conditions on earth and beyond. It's believed that this aircraft can warp time and space, therefore creating wormholes and teleportation techniques much more advanced than the Earth planet military has.

These Awacs enveloped the sky. A fleet of them had been sent by God.

Through a big live screen, we saw that we were living on Earth at a time when holistic and alternative doctors and therapists were killed, murdered, and kidnapped, sent to asylums and concentration camps to be tortured.

It was a big projection in front of our eyes of the reality of what is hidden from human beings on planet Earth.

We saw that one well-known alternative TV show that received warnings and decided to continue without consideration of these warnings is now under investigation. Another famous doctor on the big screen is put in jail.

We saw a dentist who spent his entire life researching what frequencies can do to help the body also receive a warning; he is giving all his files to a friend to keep in case something happens to him. The friend's mission is to anonymously release the documentation and the information the dentist gathered if he disappears or is killed.

A well-known bookstore uses a program to read the books before putting them for sale on the shelves. This computer program is programmed to find specific words and information concerning real news hidden from the public. That company will refuse your books but will still keep among its data your personal information, like your social security number. Your name is kept now on a blacklist by Kenney Yon.

The same is happening with websites that could bring information to the public about what those self-elected to power want to keep undisclosed. But the good news is that all this can be changed. Human thoughts are very powerful when in full alignment with the Divine inner self. This unlimited expression of the Divine self was viewed by the elite in power as a threat to their very existence because the third density has been dominated by them for a very long time on other worlds. To have a third-density world be completely free from their manipulations and feeding was something that they could not allow to happen without a fight.

But, once your Inner Divine Light is expanded, and you are connected to the Earth, imagine yourself projecting a beam of white Light from your inner self straight up to the galaxy. It will pierce the dark control grid.

It is very important to be aware that they use your own subconscious beliefs as portals into your psyche. Fear is their primary tool, and they embed fearful scenarios in the dream state to make a person susceptible to their programming. To work more quickly these days, they are arresting innocent people and giving them psychotropic drugs. Then they can induce fear.

Before time and the Universe were formed, CHADD & VIE existed in an ecstatic world of light and sound, in the existence level of Soul realms.

The physical world is but a creation of our consciousness. We, CHADD & VIE, came to help you play your role and get you back home.

We live in a Universe that was created abundantly. The idea of a shortage of anything in this life is an illusion that comes with the idea that you are less than infinite in your potential. How could the creator have created such a thing?

I, CHADD, come from Jupiter, and VIE from Venus.

Our bodies exist in a location in space and time called oneness. Currently, our location is on Earth and the Planet Oneness, so we are about to morph and teleport.

Currently, our physical carbon-based bodies are in two locations simultaneously. Our minds, however, are free to roam to different locations and even to other points in time. We are time travelers. We have our spiritual hearts activated, and we are in constant joy, peace, bliss, and continual inspiration.

We chose to come back at this specific time to be able to help you progress and ascend before 2029.

While in a coma, CHADD was taken back home to "Heaven" by the Father and his DNA reconnected to the Father and sent back with full power. DNA absorbs and transports Light. Light is a valuable source of energy that keeps biological organisms alive and healthy.

Light is transported by Love, which means that Light used for healing purposes cannot be applied by any electronic device, but only human Love energy. Nothing can replace the energy of human Love.

Your gateway to spiritual consciousness is Love. When you are attuned to the natural flow of love throughout the Universe, you will feel the natural flow of energy within yourself.

Remember, the flow of love within is critical. Tune into it; love will not let you down.

Life is only a work in progress, and the Creator can adjust at any point along the timelines.

The fabric of space is created by the love aspect of the Creator. Love is the aspect of infinite Being that provides the supportive matrix upon which all else is built. Space is no more than a concept in consciousness, and everything in consciousness is within you.

We are here to demonstrate to you the path of oneness.

We have lived many lives in many different eras – Egypt, Atlantis, and more – as high priests and Priestess.

We are two physical bodies, though one pure light of oneness. We are connected by the heart of Energy.

Our teaching is fully approved and endorsed by the Angelic forces that watch over this planet. It was always known that our teaching was to assist the evolution of the planet, which would be distorted by the Illuminati. The good will still outweigh the dark.

Freedom, peace, new technology, and harmony await all when the Illuminades have been defeated on a level most people can never have dreamed of.

We always take on the same attributes; for instance, VIE is ambulatory, and CHADD travels incognito by wheelchair. We are normal to our superior leader who created us millions of years ago.

We came before you to stand behind you and tell you something that will help you grow and survive.

Soon there will be an implosion an outer-space intergalactic black hole that will open. No one will survive unless he believes in God.

However, our journey to gain this information has been fraught with many dangers. Not everyone has believed us. Family and friends have turned against us. They feared that shadowy forces could disrupt their lives simply because they did not want us to process this.

But once full self-acceptance is gained through love and forgiveness, you do not need to be plagued by fear. On the wheel of karma, we will remain at the highest and most rewarding point.

The adversary, the ones in power, and their teachings on pursuing money, power, and fame create dominant behavior. Everything is built around hierarchy. They show themselves as indestructible; they are seriously corrupt forces that keep you in fear and teach you that the best thing in life is to accept their reality.

But you have the choice; it all depends on you. Now all of this is changing. Each of you has the choice to focus on the positive and avoid re-creating the cycles of torture and pain that have plagued you.

There is no sound in outer space. There are pulses of sonar that penetrate the spirit. Every one of the beings that are like CHADD and VIE can teleport and morph.

VIE wears Cartier jewelry made of gold. Some things never change because our styles depend on class. Trends never change when you use the highest class, which is what we choose to wear in our daily wardrobe. As an example, all the women of Venus wear the same as VIE.

CHADD du Messie is here because of VIE.

Venus contains only superior ladies, proportioned 36-24-36, 5 foot 10. All the women of Venus are of the same shape. Every Titan man desires them most. They are the superior French Women with specialty.

We are both superior in our physical appearance on earth, and men and women of the opposite sex desire us deeply.

For instance, VIE's sex appeal is superior on her planet. She is the leader of Venus, and from an intergalactic space-time continuous point of view, CHADD must not alter-wives. He must stay pure for his superior God's creation is in his seed.

Purity is very important to him although he has quite a libido that the women of Venus can't handle. They would disintegrate.

Jupiter was created billions of years ago. Men are always with other women from Venus until death parts them.

CHADD is the Creator, AKA Christ, and VIE is known as Marie-Madeleine.

We are here to introduce the Twelve Commandments.

The Twelve Commandments

1   - You shall have no other God before me.

2   - You shall not make idols.

3   - You shall not misuse the name of God.

4   - Remember the Sabbath and keep it Holy.

5   - Honor your Father and Mother.

6   - You shall not kill.

7   - You shall not commit adultery.

8   - You shall not steal.

9   - You shall not lie.

10   - You shall not covet your neighbor's wife.

11   - You shall not deprive anyone of freedom or fate. Forgive or
       forget.

12   - No one shall harness the Key to Enoch except CHADD & VIE.

God's Invitation- The Devil is a Liar

God is a color. The color is Gold suave. Once you enter the color suave, you reach the euphoria of what is a cosmic orgasm that feels like it never ends. God is inviting you at that time to join him and reach euphoria.

The rainbow of Light will then catch you and swipe you into a dance that intertwines with the matrix.

Then you reach the zero gravitational pivot point. Once these points are accessed, your body begins to float. Now we're going to fly like a bird on Earth.

Gravity does not exist. It is a figment of your imagination. We have designed a special tool that allows you to float, fly, and breathe underwater.

Don't let anything or anyone separate you from the Love of God and don't let the devil steal your joy.

The devil is a liar, and the truth is not in him. He likes to confuse. Confusion is nothing more than the devil's trick. Do not be deceived; follow what is right.

Summary

This odyssey began when VIE met CHADD in a wheelchair and felt a deep and strong connection, inexplicable. She got to know him better and became enveloped in a world of mysticism, government conspiracies, religions/cults, and upcoming prophesied events. Entered a world of lies deception, hope, and pain. Her spiritual journey began when she joined forces with her blue flame, CHADD, to bring the words of Jesus.

CHADD is a Baker-acted, drugged-up ward of the state, holds the key to the Divine wisdom and VIE brings humanity into the light of God just when it all seems lost.

Henri was a professor who lived near an Indian tribal reservation and had a son, Edward, with his wife, Martha. Edward married Ethel, and they had a son CHADD, who was diagnosed with several behavior and mental problems after his dad took him to the government hospital that his father, Edward, used at the request of the NSA.

At the age of five, they started to do testing on CHADD to understand his unique ability. Though he was never sick, CHADD was given multiple drugs at the age of five. Then Edward divorced, and during the time of Edward and Ethel's separation, he started dating a coworker named Katherine, an archon known as the harsh woman, or surnamed the Surrogate, working hand in hand with CHADD's half-brother, Paul. Katherine's son, Paul, was a sworn law enforcement officer at that time.

Paul, Carlos, and Katherine were all involved with the corrupt government. The government would take the drugs from the drug dealers in the West, send them to Miami for sale in Florida, and generate money for the government's clandestine

Chapter 1
An Epiphany

CHADD left his body and caught on to exactly what his "mother" and the doctors were doing to his temple and mental well-being at a young age.

CHADD: "They were destroying my health by being verbally abusive, implanting sicknesses into me, destroying my image. My family was brainwashed by the doctors' scare tactics and verbiage in conjunction with the flood of advertising. This could only lead to one thing: my demise."

It would have been a guarantee of certain death if he had believed everything that these doctors and family implanted into him.

He felt that his entire family should be completely ashamed and decided to write them a note.

"You all pushed me to the point of no return, left me handicapped with no car, no house that I own, no money, after so many years of institutions. Depriving me of everything, freedom, and legal rights.

"Please live your own life and keep your comments to yourself. You owe me an apology, all of you, and this is important to me. I want you to make it in front of the court of justice. Nothing less. Do not ask or harass me for money ever again. Shame on you.

"You never learn, do you? How dare you Baker Act me on Christmas Day and have me admitted to a mental hospital! Did you have a good Christmas at least while I was in a facility?"

The Florida Mental Health Act of 1971 (Florida Statute 394.451-394.47891 (2009 rev.) commonly known as the "Baker Act," allows the involuntary institutionalization and examination of an individual. The Baker Act allows for involuntary examination (what some call emergency or involuntary commitment).

Chapter 2
The Beginning of a New Life

"When I was young, I was requested to take an IQ test by the school. As a result, I was put on many prescription drugs that led me to depression and to try different forms of alcohol. Then I gave it up to become a parishioner for the Lord God. I understood who I was and what was my purpose on this Earth.

"No one seemed to take me seriously, but I wouldn't let it stop me. My father was an alcoholic, and my surrogate mother was abusive to me. She kept Baker Acting me to keep me on psychotropic drugs and under the care of these physicians who have no conscience and sold their souls to the devil for money. Thanks to my "LOVING MOTHER," the wife of my dad, I have been admitted to many, many mental places and here are a few of them: Laurel Oaks, Glen Bay, Park Side Lodge, Wuesthoff Center/Rockledge, Chateau Asylum, Rats Asylum, 6th Floor Bird Lake Hospital, Loop link Hospital, three different Waterside behavioral hospitals, South County Hospital, Oriental Florida Parkway Behavioral, DKF (Department of Kids and Family) ... just to name a few.

My brother (Katherine's son) was jealous of me, would always beat me, and never helped me, and I had no one to turn to. I discovered since then that my entire family is on it. They have all sold their souls. It is all about greed and money. For instance, my government checks have been used for years for my mother's expenses while I was kept in the back of my parents' house without towels and barely fed.

This was only when I was not in one of these hospitals or mental facilities.

One day when I felt so weak, the Father talked to me and told me to go and look for a cross with copper. This is how I met VIE and her VAJRA.

This was the beginning of my new life. Thanks for kicking me out, Mom. I am doing great even though you made VIE's life very difficult, contacting her family, whom you were not introduced to by the way, and recounting to them some lying stories and fables by taking some real facts and reporting them twisted. As you did to my lawyers, the doctors, my banker, my friends, the entire family, and more.

VIE's family did not understand that all they heard from you was lies. They had never seen a mother and a family that did not support their own. Of course, you were pleading with them as the poor mother of an insane son and described me as a mentally ill person who needed to be kept drugged. But you did not tell them that it was psychotropic drugs.

What is funny is that since I am away from all of you because you had an idea in a minute of genius to kick me out, and since I am off of psychotropic drugs, I am living finally a normal life and able to use my brain.

Now I do not have any health insurance, and no facilities want me for free. I have no more government checks, and I cannot pay doctors and fill my prescriptions. Thank God!

VIE and I entered a life of supernatural, unexplained mysteries, ghosts, monsters, and psychic phenomena, fighting fallen angels and demons. We found ourselves living in a corrupted system. After living in the custody, at the age of forty, of the DKF (Department of Kids and Family) and the State of Mickey Land, I decided to take a chance.

The corrupt government has deprived me of my disability check and continues to harass me for money. I have spent over one thousand days of my life between two asylums, both located at the border of Florida and Georgia. This has to stop now. My life has been passed between behavioral centers and hospitals. Now I have been declared competent and told that there is nothing wrong with me, and by the same doctors that had declared me incompetent!

The doctors in these types of places and this field of medicine used names like M.D. Dr. Sanity, Dr. Yong, Dr. Tragedy, Dr. Kidir, or Physician Mc Bakerer, Amkilla... and I have grace for most of these doctors.

But there will be no grace in heaven or on earth for the couple that I have named Dr. Affia and Assam Al Kalssam, The Al Kidir of the Tri-Regional Psychiatric and Associates in Orange. They run a behavioral hospital next to the dolphin park. (They go by different names, among others the Kidirs.)

They are a husband and wife here in Florida, and they have controlled my destiny and my life since 1994. For instance, I am human, and I have grace for most, like their nurse practitioner from their Tri-Regional Psychiatric Associates Center.

The reason I say I have grace is because Betsy, their nurse practitioner, gave me a drug that would kill my semen. I was disgusted by this and have since prayed for all of their souls even though I think they are a team of killers. Thank God that I memorized a PDR or Physicians' Desk Reference. I am not a pharmacist but a holistic healer, working for the institute that created a new therapy, the same therapy that helped me recover from all these years of psychotropic drugs that I was forced to ingest and even been court ordered to swallow.

I am CHADD, and I took my name back from this psychiatrist couple with the Tri-Regional Psychiatric Associates place. My name is an acronym with the spelling of CHADD. The Tri-Regional Psychiatric Center tried to steal my name, so I stole it back.

Now that I have spent over one thousand days of my life under the control of psychotropics, I am looking forward to going to court and intend to win my life back. All this is possible because of VIE. We are two gifted holistic healers sent by the Creator actually aboard our spaceship. Only a copy of us is seen by you on the planet Earth.

I have been brainwashed while under psychotropic drugs to do things that I was not aware of or did not want to do. Then I was declared incompetent and sent to mental hospitals, behavioral centers, and asylums and given more psychotropic drugs. I was kept in a foggy state when I was a holistic therapist and an expert on sound frequencies. (Though they tried hard to make me commit a reprehensible act, I have never hurt anyone, stolen, or killed anybody.) But every hospital and facility has stolen my personal belongings: a watch, gold necklace, jeans, T-shirts, and underwear. Shame on them!

Nobody knew that my consciousness was still aboard Commandant Sheran's spaceship, and I was observing everything, registering all the details of the movie they were making about VIE and me. All that to make us look bad, ridicule us, destroy our image, and make big money on us.

And funnily enough, for someone who was labeled for years incompetent, our office has been visited and my customized sound system is broken because of the great results we get from our sessions with clients.

Around three weeks after I was released from the asylum, this article from Nick Dukan was sent to VIE and CHADD to read.

Chapter 3
KAFOA the Shaman

I was sitting in a very luxurious tropical jungle with people from an island. I was offered some kava-kava in an official ceremony by Kateva.

I rapidly left my body and began to float. The vision was vivid and clear. Here is what Kafoa the Shaman is showing us:

Three days before Dr. Ceron was found dead, U.S. Government agents raided his research facility to seize a breakthrough cancer treatment called GcMAF.

The history of the suppression of medical science in America is a long one, filled with true accounts of pioneering doctors and clinicians being threatened, intimidated, and even assassinated to bury emerging cures and keep the "sick care" industry in control.

Before being found shot in the head, the pioneering medical researcher Dr. Ceron was working with Kafoa on a little-known molecule that occurs naturally in the human body. This molecule has the potential to be a universal cancer cure for many people. Dr. Ceron was working telepathically with. It has also been shown to reverse signs of autism in the vast majority of patients receiving the treatment.

The medicine man is now commenting. His voice seems distorted: "Is there a motive for the murder of pioneering cancer researchers working on a possible universal cancer cure? Of course, there is, he says, it's the most common motive in the world: MONEY.

Imagine! A cure for cancer would destroy the very profitable cancer industry. It would mean the destruction of the Cancer Society, hospitals, oncology clinics, and pharmaceutical companies. They depend on chemotherapy revenues. The key to it is the inescapable fact that conventional cancer treatments simply don't work. Patients are never cured, and they create a reliable profit stream of repeat business.

Now, would the cancer industry go as far as to murder doctors to protect its profits? Yes, it would. The industry is used to killing. It kills patients as a routine part of its business operations! Did you know that an oncologist was recently sentenced to nearly sixty years in prison for falsely diagnosing patients' cancers so that he could sell them chemotherapy treatments they didn't need?

What no doctors will ever reveal to you is that a simple ingredient could very well be the cure for all diseases. Big pharma and doctors have been keeping it away from you because it would put their billion-dollar medical industry at risk if a simple natural cure could cure you for pennies on the dollar. But when God has had enough of his children being murdered, it will be too late. My Brothers and Sisters in Christ, pray harder.

Chapter 4
The Little-Known Molecule

I, VIE had a vivid dream, and then a conversation with an Angel, searching for more clarity on this vision.

This coming Sunday during office mass the celebrant Priest will ask all the parishioners to help anyone that could be in difficulty and could be a target and killed.

The government has declared war on the Holistic doctors and has released CHADD, to use him as a part of a cover-up, holding him responsible for all the doctors killed.

I was asked to write about it. "They are going to use the fact that he has been released without prescriptions and are going to say that he must be on prescription drugs.

"They will use everything they have in their power with the collaboration of Katherine and Paul to keep him away from me and collect his social security.

"Though, they know that they used humanoid clones to manipulate his brain to a criminal mischief..."

Chapter 5
Think About it Now and Join the Forces

The Thuggees are creatures reincarnated from India and Pakistan that have infiltrated the US. They trap people in their hospitals with psychotropic drugs. They are creatures without soul that cannot create but can use your brain when you are under their power and the influence of drugs. They have no emotions and no feelings; therefore, they do not care if you suffer or die. There is no mercy when you are in their grips. You are their experiment. They worship Kali.

Vaccination shots: Your children are poisoned by shots a few hours after birth, and it kills their neurons. The older ones get Alzheimer's, diabetes, and schizophrenia.

Funnily, a French doctor, Dr. Dupuis, made an experiment when one colleague sent him his patient with Alzheimer's and schizophrenia. He began by eliminating many prescription drugs the patient was on that he found out he did not need. At the same time, he worked with a nutritionist to detox the body, and add some natural supplements to oxygenate the body and nourish the cells. A couple of months later the patient recovered total clarity of mind and health too.

Many doctors have been found dead, shot, disposed of in rivers, and mysterious deaths.

Colorado's Animas River turns yellow with pollution, which a geophysicist warned of before it appeared.

Yosemite National Park is infested by plague and is beginning to infest visitors.

What else do you need? Think about it before you judge the Lightworkers. Are you going to awaken and be part of the awakened people? Are you going to join them and save the planet and your children? Or are you going to surrender your life to the dark and fallen Angels?

Because if parents will all join forces as in another country, you would not have to go through these vaccinations anymore.

Parents of all autistic children in the South Pacific manifested in hospitals all over the country until the Health Minister backed down and decided to leave the choice of vaccinations to the parents.

Join forces and claim the truth about the doctors' deaths.

Join forces and manifest against the Colorado River's pollution.

Join forces and fight plant disease.

Chapter 6
The Culture War

The vaccine war taking place in America today is a war pursued by some of the most irrational and intellectually dishonest Big Pharma runners, reporters and bloggers ever witnessed in recent memory. These people ignore real science and use dishonest tactics of fear and social shaming, lying about scientific facts to bewitch informed parents and attempting to outlaw those who ask intelligent, scientific questions concerning vaccine safety.

This way, doctors, health regulators, lawmakers, and vaccine patent owners are walking human beings down the path of medical crimes against humanity, as once was witnessed carried out by scientists under the Nazis.

There is a new video that explains these dark parallels between today's vaccine culture war and the Nazi-era medical crimes against humanity. Both are predicated on the totalitarian belief that the government owns your body and can therefore tell you what to do with it. (www.naturalnews.com).

Chapter 7
The Cancer "Industry" for Profit

Cancer is an industry and an implanted disease for profit. Doctors, pharmaceutical companies, hospitals, and shareholders of the industry profit every time one patient agrees to conventional treatment. It normally involves injecting chemotherapy toxins into the body, with ionizing radiation or, in some cruel cases, cutting off body parts.

The cost of a single treatment today can be $1,000,000.

For 25 years, D. Dickson was studying cancer patients and came to a horrifying conclusion.

It is little known that science is covering up or ignoring this.

Most patients who have died of cancer died of malnutrition.

Chemotherapy is assisted suicide. The majority of patients die of malnutrition. While chemotherapy destroys the immune system, cells suck all nutrients from the blood and weaken the body, which is no longer able to defend itself against infections.

Modern medicine has at its disposal an elixir, a cure-all, and the truth about cancer is tactfully hidden. The majority of cancer patients die of chemotherapy. Chemotherapy does not remove lung cancer, colon cancer, or breast cancer. This fact has been documented for more than a decade, but doctors still stubbornly use chemotherapy for these tumors.

Chapter 8
Infecting an Island with Cancer

CHADD and I heard about Dr. Cornerous, that's right, Cornerous, who was sponsored by the Stonefellas Institute to conduct experiments on an isolated island. He infected Puerta Bella citizens with cancer cells, presumably to study the effects. Fifteen of them died.

So, we sent one of our scientists to travel to Puerta Bella, and he came back terribly shocked with this information.

What's most obvious is that the accusations stem from a note Dr. Cornerous allegedly wrote:

"The Porta Bellas are most degenerated, the dirtiest, laziest, and thievish race of humans ever to inhabit this Planet... I have done whatever I could to further the process of extermination by killing off eight and transplanting cancer into several more... All these physicians take delight in the abuse and torture of the unlucky subjects."

And this man who seems determined to kill Puerta Bella through a cancer infestation would not seem a suitable candidate to be elected by the country to be in charge of chemical warfare projects and receive a seat on the Atomic Energy Commission, right?

But that is exactly what happened. And of course, any shocking documentation of what happened during his chemical warfare period probably has been destroyed by now.

Chapter 9
Proof that the Devil exists

Right now, CHADD has proof that the devil exists in many people. Therefore, Satan hides in many different vessels or bodies of different people.

"I have proof by staring the devil in his eyes. I have proof by looking into their eyes that the devils are the Al Kalssam.

They are with the Tri-Regional Psychiatric Associates and al Qaeda to take over the world.

My other name is Christ, and I work for the Bio- -Institute under the name of CHADD du Messie.

I have taken a picture of Antonio Library; he is connected directly to the Al Kalssam family. Therefore, you must drop to your knees and worship God."

Chapter 10
A Call Out from CHADD

"Lord my God, I call out by day at night, I cry aloud in your presence. Let my prayers come before you; incline your ear to my cry. For my soul is filled with trouble. My life dwells near the end. I am reckoned with those who go down to the pit. I am weak, without strength! My coach is among the dead, with the slain who lie in the grave. You remember them no more; they are cut off from your care. You plunge me into the bottom of the pit into the darkness. Your wrath lies heavy upon me. All your waves crash over me. Selah."

I cannot escape. My eyes grow dim from trouble. All day I call on you; I stretch out my hands to you.

Christ, do the shade arise and praise you? Know that I am your savior. I am Christ with the God Duo of Orlando.

I have been crucified, and after 2000 years I am here to get my children back. Do not be ignorant or stubborn for I am the chosen one. But I cry out to you and pray to my father.

Oh! Lord my prayer comes out before you. Thank you for not rejecting me, O Lord. I am mortally afflicted since youth; lifeless, I suffer the terrible blows your wrath has swept over me. Your terrors have reduced me to silence...

O Lord! Show your deeds to your Servants. Your Glory to their children.

The day of worship is going to be every Saturday up until Armageddon.

Prosper from the work of our hands. Lord avenging God shine forth. Rise, judge the earth, and give the proud what they deserve.

Chapter 11
We Came here to Assist You Grow Spiritually

We are called the God Duo and are here to assist you in continuing your journey through the fourth dimension. Remember to hold the intention of creating a clear portal that unites the third and fourth dimensions with the fifth dimension.

The third dimension is a holographic projection. It is such an effective hologram that most people believe that it is real. It is real because your third-dimensional form is also a holographic projection.

The true, fifth-dimensional representation of Planet Earth and all its inhabitants is projected through the fourth-dimensional light rays. This astral light ray is cast onto the third-dimensional screen to create the holographic reality of the third-dimensional Earth.

Anger is a way of pushing away something too frightening to address. When the dark spirits from 3D become frightened, they often become angry.

It is the awakened ones who will clear the portals through the astral fourth dimension and into the fifth dimension of unconditional love and multidimensional light.

Humanity has prime responsibility for the darkness that is stored within the fourth-dimensional Astral Plane. Therefore, humanity must clear this darkness, this fear.

Those who still live in darkness have also forgotten that Gaia, our planet Earth, is a FREE WILL planet

These dark beings who live in anger and for the need of power over others are the ones who taint Gaia's aura.

They are not sufficiently evolved and do not live by Gaia's Law of Cause and Effect.

By not taking responsibility for their actions, they are depriving themselves of the enjoyment of the return of the energy fields sent out into the world.

As they have victimized others, they have also victimized themselves. These beings full of anger feel like victims because they are lost in their darkness.

Therefore, any manner in which these dark ones have decreased the free will of others will soon return to them. The boomerang effect!

Fairness is not a component of the ascension. If their actions have not returned to them yet, it is because there is a greater plan in operation.

Ascension is the potential to unconditionally love. A way to forgive and accept all life. But beloved ones, your challenge is so much more difficult than theirs but worth it.

Everyone creates his reality with his every thought and emotion. If anyone is having difficulty with that challenge, you should assist and not judge him.

To be able to travel through the inter-dimensional portal, which is the ascension portal that you are creating and almost completed, it is important to let go of the attachment to the third-dimensional reactions.

While moving through each sub-plane of the fourth-dimensional astral plane, all have greatly volunteered for the challenge and the task of assisting and guiding others and know that it will not be simple. And everyone needs to fully connect to his fifth-dimensional self.

Chapter 12
An Ice Cream with my "Father's Wife" The Surrogate

Out of the blue appeared this young girl in the seat in front of CHADD. She had a big smile and an intense look in her striking blue eyes. She sat there staring at him for a good ten minutes. She put CHADD in a trance state. He suddenly began to talk out loud:

"When I was young, I had to go out for ice cream. I was screaming because I was being Baker Acted by my mother, a surrogate, and admitted to Park Side Lodge in Kissimmee, Florida.

Since the age of 13, I went to a camp called Park Side Lodge in Kissimmee, Florida, which is no different than the assisted living facility called "Montemple" where I was admitted later on.

I had to drink juice containing red dye 40, to which I am allergic, in every one of the facilities, hospitals, and camps. I was told to "drink the juice and pop the pills." There was no way to get away. Keep in mind that these were psychotropic." Then the girl vanished, saying, "Remembering traumatic events is healing you. Love you."

Chapter 13

Received from Ezra

God's breath of life, one question remains, however! How can evolution and the physical Universe account for the spiritual or rational nature of humankind?

I, CHADD, received from Ezra last night the wisdom "He returned from exile" about Asmodeus the Thug.

Sarah lost seven husbands, each killed in turn on his wedding night by the demon – Thug- Asmodeus. God heard the prayers of Tobit and Sarah and sent them the Angel Raphael in disguise to help them both.

When Tobiah was attacked by a large fish as he bathed, Raphael ordered him to seize it and remove its gall, heart, and liver because they make useful medicines. Later, at Raphael's urging, Tobiah married Sarah and used the fish's heart and liver to drive Asmodeus from the bridal chamber.

Returning to Nineveh with his wife and his father's money, Tobiah rubbed the fish's gall into his eyes and cured them. Finally, Raphael revealed his true identity and returned to heaven. Tobit then uttered his beautiful hymn of praise. Before dying, Tobit buried his father and mother. He and his family departed for Media, where he later learned that the destruction of Nineveh had taken place.

I saw in a premonition something very disturbing. VIE was choked by Mooky at her computer when typing and bringing the news to you. Mooky is a demon that was cast upon VIE by the Al Kidir.

We are a danger to them. We are in a battle with the demonic beings while fighting for our boss to come back to earth.

I am clairsentient, clairvoyant and I have telekinesis. I can see into the future, into the past, and the present. I can make predictions like Nostradamus and can prove it through earthly transitions such as hurricanes and lightning storms, hail storms, and windstorms, and sometimes even predicting friends' deaths, which leaves me feeling guilty.

I have a spiritual connection to two dimensions, Earth, and heaven.

Sometimes it scares the hell out of me, but the clear message that I have to give you today is that I have cornered the devil in Orlando.

Chapter 14
A prayer to God, The Law Giver

"Happy are those whose way is blameless, who walk by the teaching of the Lord. Happy are those who observe God's decrees, who seek the Lord with all their heart. They do no wrong; they walk in God's ways.

"I will not be ashamed to ponder all of your twelve commandments. I will praise you with a sincere heart; I will keep your laws. Do not leave us alone." (Psalm 119)

CHADD expresses himself now: As the God Duo, our lives are always at risk, but I do not forget your teaching, VIE. The wicked have set snares for me, but from your precepts, I do not stray.

Your decrees are my heritage forever. They are the joy of my heart. They are my reward forever. Selah!

I hate every hypocrite, but God's teaching I love.

You are my refuge and shield. In your word, I hope.

I must take this time to describe what it's like to have survived so many assassination attempts that now I hand my entire plate to the sky and surrender all I have to the one and only Creator, the Messiah, Jehovah, which is the God Duo team.

Crash course and brain surgery.

During my garage day, I was once a basket-case, and then I met this wonderful light I call Whistle Teeth.

As my premonitions continue nightly through powerful visions and dreams, deathly silence is imperative to me.

I reach my ultimate REM (rapid eye movement), and my gift shines forth the next day. This is what I call premonition and psychic ability.

Since I met VIE, I am not scared of it anymore. But I understand my power now, and all I have to say to you readers is that gravity is painful.

I like to float above all the people and above Florida and all my dreams. And as we, CHADD and VIE, see southwest Florida as a vortex/port we tell you:

Do not stop searching day and night and do not settle until you find the mysteries of the light of the kingdom, which will cleanse you and make you rarefied Light. That will lead you into the Light- Kingdom.

Renounce the entire world and all matter within it and its concerns and all its sins and in general all associations with it, that you may be deserving of the mysteries of Light and be delivered from all chastisements which are in the judgments.

Christ is telling us that we are not to share in the Glory and fame of the powers of Earth. These powers and glories are associated with the lower archons, and these alignments only build worldly attachments that become more and more difficult to break.

You are to seek association with the Orders of Light instead of the power games of the earth.

This era that we live in is an era of greed, genocide, and control of human beings under the Anunnaki. The "Illuminades." They deprive all souls except those of their race of most everything. They poison children at birth with vaccinations that contain mercury and aluminum when they know that babies and small children cannot reject it from their bodies. It creates autism, destroys the neurons, and causes many other disabilities.

Chapter 15
Shocking and Vile Inhuman Experiments

Many parents don't realize that when they purchase vaccines for their babies, the cost is taxed, and the money goes into a special fund to compensate them if and when those vaccines seriously injure or kill their babies. Three years ago, more than $2.5 billion was paid out for thousands of injuries and deaths caused by vaccines. Numerous cases are still pending. Awards were issued for permanent injuries such as learning disabilities, seizure disorders, mental retardation, paralysis, and numerous deaths, including many that were initially misclassified as sudden infant death syndrome.

A shocking amount of vile, inhumane, and horrible experiments on humans without their consent and often without their knowledge.

Glyphosate is another form of poisoning. It is an herbicide particularly effective against perennial weeds. The point is to kill unwanted plants. Like all chemicals toxic to animals and humans, Glyphosate causes extreme disruption of the microbe's function and life processes and is one of the new widely used broad-spectrum herbicides. It accounts for around five percent of the global herbicide market. Pig (France) and rat had skeletal defects. Dogs and cats exposed to the products have experienced drooling, vomiting, diarrhea, and even have died.

As proof, the dog Max walked on it and got paralyzed. He fell on the floor and could not walk. Luckily, he was treated with holistic Light and energy and recovered while Sophie the cat could not get attention on time and died of it, totally paralyzed.

Chapter 16
Another Vision Given to Us

And the visions continue. These are deadly visions. Now we see deadly chemical sprays used on American cities by their Government. As The God Duo, we are in oneness and CHADD, and I see the same visions at the same time. The same dreams also.

The country always is inclined to test out the most unpleasant or serious things that could happen in a situation by getting to them first. With the advent of a conspiracy of biochemical warfare in this century, a global movement of people in key control places conducted a series of warfare simulations upon our cities to see how the effects would play out in the event of an actual chemical attack.

They conducted the following air strikes/naval attacks: released a whooping cough virus on Samba Bay, using boats, and caused a whooping cough epidemic. Twelve people died. They sprayed San Alamo with bacterial pathogens and as a consequence, many citizens developed pneumonia. In the Everglades and Avalon Park, one of the governing branches in control released millions of mosquitoes in the hopes they would spread yellow fever and dengue fever. The swarm left Americans struggling with fevers, typhoid, respiratory problems, and the worst, stillborn children.

Even worse was that after the mosquitoes, the conspirators came in disguise as public health workers.

While giving "assistance" to the victims, their secret intention was to study and chart the long-term effects of all the illnesses the victims were suffering from.

It is because of our powerful abilities that the Creator has invited us to be present with you, as we represent the shifts taking place within all humanity and the Earth, even within the universe of the Creator.

You are living in a world of subliminal messages and psychotropic, psychic, electronic, and electromagnetic effects.

You are being bombarded with subliminal messages that dictate you to go and eat junk food with pesticides and full of fillers, grease, and MSG. I can say that I witnessed my father's dog's painful death from cancer due to all the poisons and toxic junk foods he was fed.

Like the weight-loss industry that makes a billion per year.

After you have been bombarded with these food suggestions, you get sick and reach for the physicians and hospitals that you are supposed to trust.

Don't they have college degrees? Aren't they Ph.D.s and MDs?

Then you receive a prescription and buy the prescribed drugs. Then there is another prescription that you have to buy and another one to counter the side effects of the previous drugs that were supposed to correct the illness, and it goes on and on.

Then suddenly you become sick from the ingestion of these drugs that are poison to the body. You develop Alzheimer's, cancer... and you need to get surgery. Now, the hospital begins to get money from you also.

Human population control! Welcome to the mental control of the human population.

For instance, when the governments decide that there are too many humans on the planet they come up with a new disease like AIDS, auto immune deficiency syndrome.

That disease was created in 1985 by the governments of the New World Order (NOW). The institute has concluded scientifically by our research that this is a fact.

In 1985, a steward who was very perverted and into bestiality contracted the disease from a monkey and then had sex with men and women.

This man was put on psychotropic drugs then brain-manipulated by the government to sleep with a monkey, then as many men and women as he could. Thereafter, the government created a pill that was supposed to cure HIV.

Understand that all diseases have been created by our governments to raise more money for the New World Order, NWO.

Chapter 17
A Team of Famous Reincarnated Scientists

In the Institute, we have many scientists who even control the weather just like the Navy, who are famous scientists who reincarnated to be part of our team and join our institute to erase all diseases with the creation of our new therapy, created by me, VIE. Therapy is greatly needed to bridge the gap of the new Era.

Remember that we are from a superior race, and we came to help the planet win back its freedom and control.

Therefore, we do not need Congress to run the world, but we do need free energy from Nikola Tesla. The world is one, without any congresses or governments. Therefore, God can take over when there is free energy, no more war, murder, suicide, security, jails, prisons or courts, police, or sheriffs.

God is the only judge. God eliminated all these jobs, and the God Duo prevails.

If the world had no Congress, there would be no war, and no money; it would be a free world. It would consist of free bread, wine, and groceries, without any disease, and free will for all. Disease and poverty do not exist. The Creator did not create limitations; he wants us to enjoy life.

We would all get along, and there would be no need for medications, physicians, doctors, hospitals, mental facilities, sheriffs, and police.

Welcome to the free society.

But we still have a problem. The world, Earth, is going to suffer a great flood due to global warming because of automobiles and countries like China that do not care about the atmospheric pollutants eating up the earth. But you are as just as guilty as all of us unless you drive a green car, which is environmentally friendly.

This means the Earth needs Gods in mission.

This earth was pure when God created it, but congressmen and presidents eventually polluted the earth for monetary gains.

This is stabbing yourself in the back. Impurities and impurities come from every one of us. We all have polluted the earth. The polar caps are melting. This is going to cause a new ice age. We have already almost lost the polar bear. It has nowhere to live in the polar caps.

Chapter 18
Our Communication with God

God gives us some jokes. God jokes on the earth for the animals.

Duck-billed platypus. It is God's sense of humor! Therefore, you must listen to us. God is telling us many things.

The Anunnaki rule the earth. The world will end in the year 2029. The angels have discussed this with the God Duo; there is no reversing it.

We are just messengers of God. It is up to you to make it before the end of time.

Good luck and once again we can pray about it. Accept God as your Lord and your Savior. Confess and ask him to forgive you for your sins.

Now you can see that Jesus is, was, and always be King. Accept him with all your heart. Dr. Youth, do you remember when you said, "We will not elect a king," talking about your King in your cult? Well! We do.

Chapter 19
Sent by the Pleiadians and the Herkimer Diamond

We, CHADD & VIE, were sent to the Pleiades a millennium ago in another era, another epoch, long before humankind's current civilization.

The Pleiades as a planet was very advanced, somewhat similar to Earth in its level of advancement. Yet it was not an exact duplicate. The languages, the number of inhabitants, and also the way that people were dealing with the environment were different. There was no misuse and abuse of the environment on the Pleiades.

We were received and accepted on the Pleiades with great honor. Unlike as it has been on earth, where we have been Baker Acted, intoxicated, bruised, beaten, hospitalized, and even poisoned by the Al Kalssam, Betsy, and the system.

Exhausted by all these, we found ourselves sucked into a vortex, like a vacuum cleaner, by a rainbow spiral and found ourselves on a racing track chasing the Al Kalssam. Their faces were shape-shifting, and they were sweating a lot. We had racing cars with more advanced technologies than the Pakistani couple had. They knew we would win and catch them. All around us and on the racing track we could observe the military in jeeps and ambulances ready to take us to a camp, to shoot us up with psychotropic drugs.

But the beauty of Herkimer Diamond took us down in a hole into a place that defies gravity and logic. The energies of these stones allowed us to the entrance and exit via a crystal portal. It took us down a road between worlds and through a looking glass into a place of dimensional fluid travel, allowing us to see with clarity, activating healing, and clearing all psychic attacks and psychic debris, clearing the electromagnetic negative pollution that was attached to us.

We saw that you enter a promised time when the limited perception of your humanness merges with the cast and all-knowing Spirit of Light, coming together and merging and then remerging into something much more. We saw the Pakistani couple, Doctors Al Kalssam Kidir, auctioning off in the South our white Japanese car. Then we saw the previous owner, a woman, repossessing the car. The white Japanese car was sold to us by Fabrosio from Sicily.

By the way, we encountered him once after in a restaurant. He could not believe his eyes and was so scared because he had destroyed my credit and left me without transportation. They all contributed to it. Everyone made money on it: Fabrosio, the owner, and the insurance company, all except me.

We could observe the complete team at work. The car was sold to me by Fabrosio, but he knew that Paolina was still the owner. Then the Al Kalsam Kidir auctioned it, and everyone involved made money, except me who still owed to the loan company.

Then the loan company repossessed it and auctioned it again for less than what CHADD "owed them."

Chapter 20
Human Beings and the Chrysalis Shifts

In the big holographic screen, we saw clearly that human beings right now feel like caterpillars in the early cocoon stage.

The chrysalis shifts, and the cocoon around you thickens and hardens. There is no way out. You are confined in a prison of your thinking. With our brains trained by the concept of linear time, we think of ourselves as being stuck in one location in space and in one position in time. In reality, beings exist in an all-encompassing Here and Now, and we are facets of infinite beings. Therefore, all locations and all times can be reached just by transferring one's focus to a different place.

The Caterpillar must walk into a time of complete trust and surrender to the Father.

This is why you need to be anointed. Then, surrender what you think are your limitations to the divine glow within you. Surrendering is trusting! Your soul pushes you through that tiny hole into a higher light.

Chapter 21
Antibiotic Drugs & Pollutants to Kill

Now, this is advice for your own sake. Please, for your own sake, wake up! Look around you. Look at nature, humans, and animals that are dying with pesticides. Look at the sky that is polluted with chemtrails, automobiles gas, and more. Look at the rivers polluted by antibiotics and other drugs, and the oceans that are also polluted.

Some other areas of the exercise of control on the planet Earth are related to radar-like devices that change energy fields around the planet. These have been used in military encounters.

The chemtrails' purpose is related to holding and keeping a certain lower frequency among the population so that the people are more susceptible to control.

Believe us, we know what we are talking about. We are experts on Light and sound and work these frequencies to re-balance the body at the Institute of Light and Sound.

If there are any irritants in your energy field, like glyphosate, then you find it harder to raise your spiritual light quotient. Because your immune system becomes challenged, you need to use the energies to fight off the immune attacks.

The future will be a slow awareness change of connecting the dots. It will lead to other awareness. In the process, poverty and disease will diminish. Social issues will become more balanced as there will be more tolerance at a higher level.

From your seed parents, the Pleiadians, who love you beyond measure, the time capsules are opening. They are pouring into you the energy of a catalytic realignment of consciousness.

They have watched you deal with what is still dark on the planet and see how much your heart hurts. They are silent because free choice is yours alone.

This is going to take some time, but you have opened a door, and you are going to have a revelation of what it is all about.

Chapter 22
Be Consistent and Remember

We ask you to be consistent in meditation and prayer. When you are consistent, you will gain clarity about the steps that are needed to achieve what you want most in life.

Find and bring back the missing pieces of you that you have lost and that contribute to the feeling you are having. Ask them to cleanly repair all of these pieces and request that they fully integrate them within you. Be grateful.

Remember, meditation cultivates mental stability, depth, and openness, and all of these are needed to see through the most powerful illusion.

Chapter 23
Dissolving the Veil

The first step in dissolving the veil is to know, to believe, to accept that there is more.

An ancient Native American Indian prophecy states, "When the Blue Star Kachina makes its appearance in the heavens, the Fifth World will emerge."

This will be the Day of Purification. The Hopi name for the star Sirius is Blue Star Kachina. It will come when the Saquasohuh (Blue Star) Kachina dances in the plaza and removes its mask. The Blue Kachinas are aliens.

It's a quest to find answers to the greater truth of who we are and why we are here. Something in our souls tells us that change is happening on a global consciousness level. The blue frequency is part of that.

Sirius is the rebirth of consciousness. Blue links to higher future frequencies of consciousness as we spiral up through the patterns of Sacred Geometry.

Our consciousness hologram ends out of the blue and into the black.

Blue is the color of electricity, our reality as a bipolar electromagnetic energy grid program. Blue, allegedly an alien race that seeded this reality, is sometimes linked to the Pleiades or Sirius (Isis) blue galaxies, blue chakra, and blue ray in the ascended master pantheon of teachers.

I, VIE, am the expert on sacred geometry who will heal you and guide you into your Spiritual Life purpose. Blue Flame is the expert on sound and frequencies and uses them to re-balance your body.

If you suspect that your subconscious mind may be harboring inappropriate vows, you can release them quite simply by conscious effort. You were programmed and guided to think in a certain way and took some vows in the past that now keep you in poverty.

Enter a quiet state and make this statement that a friend of mine experimented with. It works.

"I now renounce and release all vows that I have taken which have outlived their purpose and which now limit my growth potential. I reclaim my freedom given to me by the creator at birth and declare such vows renounced and released as of now. I replace old vows with the knowing that I am loved and that I am Love."

Repeat it two or more times, adding feeling and meaning each time. Continue this statement until you feel truly liberated. Do it for twenty-one consecutive days and see what will happen.

The human condition is fear-based. To get over the fear-based condition, you need to understand the purpose of prayers and the spacing of the words there.

Now you have the Lord's Prayer as given by Jesus in the mountain and most people do it very fast, but if you say it and pause between the words, you will get another feeling; another presence comes.

You are now moving through a state of preparedness for a dynamic health increase and a rejuvenation of your body.

Many deaths are happening now only because in the dying process is alignment achieved quickly. But dying is not necessary; it is only an option that some are choosing rather than moving into alignment physically.

Never forget that you are eternal and immortal. Your physical body is a temporary temple in which a divine facet of God dwells.

Many today are beginning to awaken and are searching for a way to grow spiritually and find their purpose in their life.

This awakening seems to come with a lot of stress, anxiety, and depression that you do not understand. Therefore, people think that Reiki is their holistic way out.

Reiki is good for releasing stress and depression and helping the body to self-heal, but it can't reconnect the DNA and can't replace the work of sound frequencies and Light with sacred geometry that are necessary to achieve the reconnection of the body, mind, and spirit. It does not work on meridians either. This work requires someone who has been prepared and trained out of this dimension and has the transformation and vibrational energy for it.

Empower yourself through Divine connection.

Chapter 24
Abortion and Decisions You Take

Children are gifts from God. Abortion is a big responsibility to take, sometimes necessary due to health issues, but other than that it is a big responsibility, for one big reason; a fetus is a human being waiting to be born.

Many think that sending energy and thought within the consciousness upon earth can bring changes, but this consciousness is only approachable if you are aware of the reality that you are more than just human.

Many are in a way disconnected from this consciousness, human-wise — not spiritual but human-wise — as their belief systems have placed a block or a veil between their connections to this consciousness and human awareness.

Many think that the entire world is under the control of the matrix, the dark forces, which is true in a way, but yet they also make choices and give control to certain forces upon earth in what may seem a small way or small direction but still influences what is happening on earth. You all consider human life to be important; you see war as some type of atrocity, rape, and other violent acts as not acceptable. But let us start where humans begin.

Many among you have thought about when human life begins, where a soul enters the body, and wondered about what happens from the moment you are born, and the moment the soul enters the body.

A lot consider human life to begin at conception, while others that life begins at birth.

The Earth is a place of rules within physical reality but sometimes rules also advance chaos.

Many choices human beings make on the human level will only affect the human level. It does not assist on the spiritual level in ways you would like to see happening. It does not assist in awakening the ones who are still called asleep, unaware of their totality of being.

Even so, changes can be small and become important changes or fade away within the human creation of reality. There is nothing that you say or do that can change that.

See choices, even though they may seem small, as having an effect, not just on your reality, but the reality.

Free will comes with the responsibility of free will. Look at what is happening in the justice system.

You must reclaim your rights and ask for the laws to be applied. It is your duty.

Court "justice" has the right to life and death. But Laws must be correctly applied. The Fifth Amendment also.

Because no matter how much you think the dark forces are in control, you still can make your own choices in some way on a human level. You still have to do your part and re-establish the truth.

Every person can decipher right from wrong and make decisions that will affect his or her future. God planted this in our minds, and he expects us to make the right decision.

This is called having a conscience.

And we, as the God Duo, say that if we did not have a conscience and acted based on impulse, we would have known that God was not seeded in our minds.

Common sense should tell the judges that CHADD has a conscience. He carries the cross around his neck and tries to end every conversation with these simple words: "God bless you" or "Have a blessed day."

Keep in mind that this plants a seed that can only grow with its prayers for these people, regardless of how badly some of them have hurt him. Even the prosecutors and the probation officers he prays for daily.

We feel that they hide behind the Universal Church for legal reasons, which is not our forte. CHADD hides behind God and lives right according to God's laws.

Now that the Twelve Commandments have been cast upon the earth, CHADD feels much better about that. He can turn the page. He says:

"My prayers for myself are that I am exonerated and pardoned, which Biblically means forgiven, and can go on with my life from here.

"Start my family, and church, and find a new place to live where I will be more accepted.

"I am a changed man who works for the Lord through the Universal Life Church, and I have found that these credentials are worthless. So, what I am saying is that courts have no place in heaven, and they will burn in hell.

"These people will burn in hell for not following God's commands.

"I am honored to have VIE protect me money-wise; I know that she is an instrument of God. She is one of his children, and He rewards her with the necessities through the Institute."

There is no license in behavioral decision-making for this goes back or you are programmed through the cognitive decisions that you make in your life.

We all know right from wrong, and none of us have the judgment to overrule God.

We know that some choices are also forced by the human reality, and this is what makes the human reality a very difficult place to find the free will that is available to humans.

In a way, beliefs or attachments, religions, and certain thought systems available at this moment might be only part of the truth – or no truth at all – and letting humans be influenced by certain feelings about their belief systems can influence humans making choices for human beings at that moment.

As a human, you do not have the advantage of full knowledge of all the effects of your choices, so it is important to realize that you have to use everything available to you to make choices that can affect so many around you.

Jesus was the first soul created, and he chose to elevate humanity. He did not choose to lower his vibration so that his life could be viewed in a way as a criminal. This was not part of the original plan.

He planned to bring the Glory and help people with ascension, to help free the world from the dark, and bring the Light to help people, so that people would know that they are part of the Creator, and people would find enlightenment.

The Magi at the time of the first coming of Jesus knew this event was at hand because they were aware of the continuous unfolding of time and circumstances for all mankind across the millennia. They knew it at the time of the last alignment with the galactic center, which saw the fall in consciousness in Atlantis.

Chapter 25
The Story of the Three Wise Men, the Magi

Most are aware of the Magi through the story of the three wise men. The term "magus" means seer.

The problem today with the human condition as we know it is that you are not taught that you are infinite and eternal beings. You are not taught all the abilities you have, so you cannot participate or have a conscious recognition and awareness of your true whole being within the entire dimension of the universe. A few of you have begun to feel, see, or otherwise experience a few of these energy forms, but you have no real education in acceptance of what were considered to be miraculous abilities.

Instead, those who have gifted insights or talents are taught how not to use them to conform to a level of living that is "socially" acceptable. Like the kids today who are labeled ADD/Bipolar...and put finally into a foggy state with drugs that have terrible side effects that ruin the neurons. They have miraculous abilities. So, when they are not put on drugs at a young age by the system, they are arrested for minor felonies and put on psychotropic drugs once in jail.

This is a great injustice to mankind, and it is done at the hands of other men by the actual system in control that self-elects to power and puts itself into key places (Illuminati, the illuminades, archon, avatar, reptilian) on purpose to instill an aversion to anything new or different to maintain the status quo. That is one of the main reasons that fear has guided so many lives into disparaging thoughts and ruinous behavior. Manipulation of the human brain.

Not always have the powers been able to harness and shackle mankind. There have been many notable visionaries throughout the ages, like the Magi, who have protected and passed down the truth regarding mankind's real potential. They were much more than just the three Kings of Bible fame.

Most of you are aware of the Magi through the story of the "Three Wise Men" who traveled to visit Jesus when he was born, but few are aware of who they were.

The term magus means seer, someone who can enter into other dimensions. And we all have this ability; we just do not remember.

The Magi came to Earth at the time of the last alignment with the galactic center some 12,500 years ago, the time of the fall of Atlantis, and they have continued to return to protect and carry forward knowledge that is required for Ascension.

Whenever the possibility of a Golden Age on Earth emerged, they began to bring these secrets forth, only to hide them again when the dark forces that have been in control of consciousness on the planet since the time of Atlantis destroyed the plans.

So, what is not recognized in the Bible concerning the Magi is that they were not just bringing gifts of precious aromatic herbs and precious metals.

They brought secret knowledge on scrolls to be given to those who would teach the young Jesus, to prepare him for his work.

And they have continued to protect those secrets and all of the skills and abilities we have that go along with that. That is why we cannot participate or have conscious recognition and awareness of our whole true self within the entire dimension of the universe.

Chapter 26
How the Dark Attacks

The person who knows that they have attained a higher vibration is not as guarded because they think they are doing all they need to do and that they can protect themselves.

They feel that they are on the right path, and they are not as aware of the attack, or, perhaps, that there is a wake of darkness around them.

They do not become aware of it because they are concentrating more on where their heart is leading them.

On a higher dimension, the dark has a different sense-impression in (your) energy and so until an individual starts to recognize that, he can fall into a trap, or the dark will lure him in.

So, if you are like CHADD and have been into psychotropic prescription drugs, they attack you and then manipulate you and your brain, and you become the subject of the state.

They essentially reprogrammed humans to be like them: fearful, petty, dishonest, brutal, murderous, unforgiving, punishing...This ensured that humans would be easy to manage as an energetic food source for thousands of years.

Chapter 27

The Knights Templar and the Gothic Cathedrals

The Templar Knights emerged around 1119 with powerful protection from the Catholic Church and became an extraordinary force for transformation in Europe. They became very wealthy and also brought forth mechanisms to protect pilgrims of any type, whether they were traveling to the Holy Land or elsewhere. They also transformed the nature of trade within Europe.

What is not very well known is that these individuals were deeply spiritual, deeply mystical men who were responsible for the building of the Gothic cathedrals in Europe, for purposes that, for the most part, are completely unknown to the public (like Chartres Cathedral in France that is a focus for the heart chakra and is located where two important ley lines cross).

Even though these imposing buildings are seen to be great bastions of the Catholic Church, they were built on ancient energy sites well known to the Druids and those who went before them, and they represented powerful tools for initiation and growth.

The legacy of the Knights Templar lives to this day, though groups bearing their name bear little connection to the original group. The Knights Templar has been thoroughly misunderstood by history. It is understood that they began their journey by spending some years in Jerusalem, digging in the area of Solomon's Temple. What they uncovered and what they did with what they uncovered is not well appreciated or understood.

Moreover, what is not at all preserved is the way that this group, operating under the watchful eye and indeed the approval of the Catholic Church, actually acted to preserve great secrets of the Light that the Church itself was hell-bent upon destroying, just as it sought to destroy all evidence of the true history of the one known as Jesus, and indeed groups that followed his true teaching, such as the Cathars in Southern France.

Some acknowledge that it was the Knights Templar who was responsible for the creation of the wondrous Gothic cathedrals in Europe, particularly France and that the key cathedral created an initiation path for those seekers who sought it out, just as the great temples along the Nile had done in prior times.

The skills and secrets of the Templars were held orally; they were never written down; and these were deeply mystical, deeply spiritual men who held great knowledge and who themselves could channel, bringing forth information to others in the cosmos beyond the veiled consciousness surrounding the Planet Earth, just as these messages came to them.

Chapter 28
Atlantis and the Corruption of our Planet

I received a phone call from Ayla, and this is what I heard.

May I remind you about Atlantis and what it has to do with the planet?" And she continued...

During most of its history, Atlantean citizens were enlightened and connected with their source. They could remember their previous lives, and they understood who they were and why they were on Earth.

Many people are working hard today to make you return to the Golden Age and make it a reality and each of you may contribute.

In 10,500 B.C., a group assembled to seal information in the Hall of Records in Egypt, and with the assistance of incense from the temple altars, the priests carefully worked to cleanse the minds and alleviate the desires of the participants who enclosed knowledge in sacred places. They were being prepared to move into a state of consciousness.

But we will not be capable of comprehending the information in the Atlantean chambers until we have the necessary understanding until human beings on the planet are more spiritually developed and can interpret the concept of our reaching a higher vibrational tone.

Ancient cultures were very well aware of other worlds, and their healers often contacted this spiritual realm from whence they obtained assistance.

All humans can perceive dimensions. Classes taught in the temples were in rooms similar to mini amphitheaters. The students reclined on pillows on the floor. When class began, each student took his or her crystal and would intensely concentrate on the crystal that was in his/her hands. They were absorbing and recording the complex information the teacher was sending them.

Interest in scientific achievement slowly supplanted compassionate relationships, the sharing of resources, and the harmony with nature.

A class society evolved in which priest-scientists were extremely powerful and not always working for the benefit of humanity. Much like today.

These priests-scientists used their minds to access hidden spheres to benefit others. But in the last days, their actions were a factor in the unpleasant situation before the Fall, and most magicians used their advanced information to obtain wealth and power at the expense of others.

Then people spent more time focusing on facts and possessions, similarly, substituting machinery tools to our dependence on computers, to finally change their awareness into the physical.

As they separated from their Creator, morality declined, and anger, greed hate, envy, and crime became prevalent.

The Atlanteans went to sexual orgies. Robbery and murder also became common events. The spiritual quality of life became unimportant to them.

Before their Fall, they understood, though, that Heaven and Earth were one place, and that the Creator was everywhere and in everything.

They were focused on developing their children's natural skills and respecting their instincts. The lifestyle at that time allowed them to retain and develop their natural skills as they did not have as many distractions as we do today but were close to nature.

With the increased power of group meditation, the children were able to leave their bodies and enter into the fourth-dimensional consciousness. This allowed them to acquire increased knowledge. Sounds, incense burning, crystals, and symbols facilitated their meditation. If one becomes absorbed in music, it gives rise to a subtle sensation of tuning into higher consciousness.

There were frequent prophecies of pole shifting, devastating earthquakes, and drastic, damaging changes in the Earth, as there are today. Current weather reflects the disturbances that are flowing through the consciousness of the human race. Be careful – our future is not fixed, and we have control of our destinies.

You must believe that it is possible to avoid the terrible fate of the Atlanteans and that you can create a world in which you will all benefit from their amazing achievements.

Numerous people who are attempting to restore harmony on the planet today are using a different approach. Rather than isolating themselves, they work together to combine their positive energies for the benefit of the planet and humanity.

Still, before human beings today can retrieve the Atlantean records, they will have to fully understand themselves grow spiritually, and make the transition to a higher state of consciousness.

The Indigo and Star children already know who they are, and many of them understand their purpose here. They focus on the etheric, making it difficult to adapt to conventional discipline in classrooms and to fit into society.

Frequently these children are diagnosed in school and by the system in place with attention deficit disorder or some form of hyperactivity, which alarms those who attempt to help all young people avoid frustration and achieve balance and harmony in their lives.

This is what has happened to me, but luckily, I found help through VIE, you.

Chapter 29
Indigo and Starseed Children

It is time for parents to take charge and refuse to have their children put on drugs.

Create groups, meetings, and reunions between parents to find the best strategy to defend and protect your children and their well-being. You have freedom, and you must claim it. Claim the eleventh commandment that is yours.

Your children are simply born with more strands of DNA reconnected. They came here at this precise moment of the ascension to help the planet. They have abilities that are dormant in you. These kids are full of love. They do not deserve to be treated otherwise.

Use your common sense!

Chapter 30
Surrendering

When you surrender your personal ego and identity to God, you can rise to a space-time overlap, working with your spiritual brothers and sisters through multidimensional space and time. This is essential for the ongoing fulfillment of consciousness to be one with continuity and change within the Evolutionary Continuum.

Color and Sound

Color and Sound are the most important energy structures for the imprint embodiment of the soul form. They are modeling ground structures, which shape the visible and invisible nogah shells from all preexisting geometries. (Nogah shells surrounding the body are created by the energies of contemplation, the veils of color and sound generated around the body in contemplative ecstasy of God.)

Chapter 31
You Remember the Words of Jesus

"For false Christ and false prophets will arise and will give great signs and wonders to mislead, if possible, even the chosen ones."

Look I have forewarned you. Therefore, if people say to you, "Look!" he is in the wilderness, do not go out

"Look! he is in the chambers," do not believe it.

Because the Shepherd Jesus Christ speaks to His sheep. He tells you of the universe to come. He will collect the faithful when the heavens are fully opened, and all signs have been fulfilled. Then "the Covenant of Israel" will understand the words of Jesus:

"Immediately after the tribulation of those days the sun will be darkened, and the moon will not give its light, and the powers of heaven will be shaken. Thus, the breaking of the sixth seal."

"And only then the sign of the Son of Man will appear in heaven, and then all the tribes of the earth will beat themselves in lamentation, and they will see the Son of Man coming on the clouds of heaven with power and great glory."

"And he will send forth his angels with a great trumpet sound, and they will gather the chosen ones together from the four winds, from one extremity of the heavens to their other extremity."

At this time the righteous will understand that just as the Old Testament was the Age of the Father, and the New Testament was the Age of the Son, This New Age is the Age of the Holy Spirit.

So let us now rejoice in these words:

"Thy Kingdom come on Earth as it is in Heaven."

Chapter 32
Blasphemy Covenant of Peace

There cannot be any peace unless established by God's Covenant.

"People will speak of the scriptures, but they will not understand. Their consciousness will be crucified to the "Cross of time" so that the "Cross of transfiguration will not be able to operate within them to reveal the "Revelation" of YHWH that must come to pass to break the seals of the old age."

The Old Age and the Old and New Testaments will be replaced by the Book of Knowledge, that is, the Aquarius and Holy Spirit times. The unknown part of the Bible. The misleaders hide in churches. They take advantage of the scriptures to ask for money and donations from the Church's sheep and live rich in mansions at the detriment of the poor worshipers.

"Until the appointed time is here, mankind will war upon the earth, will sweep across the face of the earth, and destroy the holy temples and holy places that contain the Word of God.

"The collective Anti-Christ will sit in the temples of the world and will govern the covenants of man and remove the constant feature that is the word of God proclaimed as the "Living Word."

They will arouse among the nations a "holy war" based upon the abomination of a "historic covenant'" and will succeed in activating "fires and destructions."

The actual Islamic groups under the names of ISIS and Al Qaeda are invading the world, under the banner of an Islamic Holy war. Destroying and burning Christian Churches, killing Christians, desecrating cemeteries, and killing Jewish people. It is happening now. Wake up!

This is the time for the outpouring of abundance when the gates of the Heavens begin to open with a witness of Light who will appear to activate the faithful of the Living Word.

And we are observing it unfolding, from Commandant Sheran's space-shift, and bringing the actual withheld news to you human beings on planet Earth.

Then, on December 18, 2015, Jesus delivered this message:

"I am your Jesus, born Incarnate.

"It is past time for your president to realize that his denial of present-day dangers is not reassuring to the public. He is generating a sense of weakness and failure to respond to the reality of the growing insecurity his policies are generating. He is trying to manufacture his truth, but saying everything is under control does not make it so.

"This is a war taking place in the hearts, and therefore, the most difficult to fight. This enemy lies hidden behind a facade of normalcy. Political correctness is often his ally.

"You cannot overcome the evil that is in hearts until fake religious beliefs are recognized as such and conquered. Live in the Truth as to what and who your enemy is."

Chapter 33
The Keepers of the Key to the Gate of Heaven

We are now instructed by the Father to let you know that we are the gatekeepers of Heaven and inform you of the next life awaiting you.

For the one that has passed the test, you are now living the Golden Age.

You have been in a state of sleep while on Earth, and it is time for you to come home (Heaven). I am guided to tell you that the gig is up. You can't pack your bags; you can't take anything with you. For instance, money burns.

Imagine if you died today and got to a transition point, like a layover, and suddenly Jesus appeared and said to you: Who are you? He does not know who you are! Then you know that it is too late. Or is he forgiving enough and graceful enough to forgive the fact that you have been given a lifetime to know him?

Go ahead and take a dollar bill and burn it with a lighter or you can take a two-dollar bill with the image of President Jackson on it and donate it to our Institute.

If you happen to have a yin/yang on a two-dollar bill with a VAJRA on it, you have graduated and passed the test.

Imagine a golf course that is an endless green, birds surrounding you 360 degrees, singing, surrounding you with the feeling of love, inner peace, and God's embrace, like being tickled by a feather all over your body, but now your body does not exist. You have shed your shell on earth. And there is now the euphoria and peace and love and true warmth and compassion of God's love as you have made the transition and made it with us.

CHADD & VIE have finally made it, and we are all going home.

Euphoric feelings are continuous in Heaven and every second counts.

My naked feeling for every one of my readers is to deeply encourage you to cut your ties with the devil.

I have met more liars in church than anywhere else. For instance, I have seen people in church who have invited me after church to smoke crack. (I have never smoked crack.)

What type of believer do you think that you are? Is that you that I am talking to? You will recognize yourself.

Some act upon their beliefs and do the right thing according to God's Love.

Just who do you think that you are to do what you want or desire against God's Law and commandments?

It is not good for the average person to try to reach the spiritual, euphoric level of the High Priestess and Priest that we are here at the institute. For instance, you will be spiritually attacked if you try to accomplish what no one should try to accomplish. Spiritual awareness can only be received from people who have been to the other side and not through the use of LSD.

Moving about is all we do. We gather scientific information from scientific studies (but not Scientology); we are scientists and all of us are guinea pigs for the US government.

And now there is a blacklist for the institute because we have figured out Illuminades.

Times have become acidly different. All the sunlight is good for us because we are all fish and we do, as is the case with many species, all we do is try to survive, every man for himself. We move about is all we do.

It is no good to figure out what makes the US government tick. But we at the institute have figured it out, and it is all about money. Yes, money.

Now do you feel used, abused, or a target? Now you feel how I feel, being the instrument of the US government.

Have you ever put yourself above an anthill and lit it on fire?

Those ants are buried like humans by another colony of ants. The head, thorax, and abdomen are all an ant is made of. God created the ant from three specific parts, but then you have to think out of the box about the cockroach and its body.

One day I was charged by one cockroach before it could bite me inside the Backimin Asylum telekinetically transferred to an inmate with words and he went to step on it. As I heard the scrunch of his skeleton being killed, I looked down and I observed a magnet coming out of the roach's body. Then God told me the devil was going to bite me through the vessel of this roach and impregnate my vessel (body) with a new disease.

The point is there is a spirit in every living creature and all creatures should be treated equally and respectfully. "Thou shall not kill" —the sixth commandment of the twelve commandments by CHADD and VIE.

God said, "Thou shall not kill," but I committed a genocide on the ants. The mound disappeared, and another showed up three or four feet away from it. And other ants came out of it to bury the dead from the mount that was burned. Scientifically proving that we are not the only creation of God.

Another day we observed a rat poisoned by strychnine and about to die. The only part of the rat that could still move was the eyes, and I felt horrible. The eyes were very human-looking. I spoke to him very gently, and I could see the fear and the love at the same time.

I came to the Catholic faith guided by VIE; I grew up Baptist. I was instructed by my family to stay away from Catholics. The reasons were a mystery, and the unspoken only fostered more mystery and suspicion. I was told that Catholics were the group who perverted Christianity, making it into books of rules, and that they were motivated by power. Every pope was the anti-Christ, and their service was a sacrifice of flesh and blood. Then I realized that all my ancestors were Christians, and the only Christians at the time were Catholics.

I realized that I came from a traditionally Catholic-Christian family.

My eyes were completely opened when I accidentally attended the RCIA group, invited by Father Benjamin. He anointed my head, and the Holy Spirit grew in me. I was received warmly into the Catholic Church. I listened to the discussion on forgiveness and was amazed. These teachings were the exact words of Jesus, not some pope. They were scriptural lessons, not power moves. I raised my hand to ask some questions and was easily and politely answered. I asked another and realized they were countering all the falsehoods I had been taught as a Baptist. They said, "Ask anything, it will all lead back to Jesus Christ. He instituted but one church and it is here today, please join us." Which I did.

I documented myself and began to read a lot.

I learned that there is only one church founded by Christ embracing all His teachings and encompassing more than merely the Bible.

Chapter 34
Programmed to Believe that You Are Powerless

We know why you are here and that you can influence and affect your reality that is beyond your comprehension, even though you are not aware of these forces. You do not understand how the fingers move to nudge this or that person.

"Go here. Do this. Don't do that. Take the pills or you will die. Walk. Don't walk. Go to sleep. Wake up now.

Every person is treated like a robot, and you are not even aware of it.

CHADD: "I was no more than a slave and their puppet, but I was aware of it." All events are being set up. Earth is inhabited by a multitude of intelligent forces, not only by humans. There are dimensional locks that keep various life forces separated and segregated.

You have been programmed as a species to believe in your dis-empowerment through TV and the educational systems.

Humans have been used as library cards by energies that do not operate with a full understanding of the human vehicle, and this has caused an imbalance in humans. Harm is caused to humans through certain entities that are dark energies that have self-elected themselves to key places throughout the entire planet.

There is a deep seeding of cancerous ideas and thoughts on the planet. Just as there is a deep seeding of the idea of cancer and also AIDS...Right now, women are afraid of breast cancer, and men of

prostate cancer. Fear is the killer. When fear runs into your body, it reminds the chemicals that go with it to come out and fill your body. They activate a spiral and the idea of death. It is that simple.

The disease is now being spread electromagnetically. It is spread electromagnetically, drawing itself from one carrier to another with a similar pattern vibration. It involves the great currents of electricity that are all around you, generated by humans and other sources. Magnetism is of course the force that holds things together. Viruses can spread electromagnetically, so that eventually you may have an entire area infused. You have magnetic particles inside your brain as well.

You are drawn to live in a certain town because of karma and the vibrations of the rest of the people. That is why you are impelled to relocate and move.

Today there are very few locations on the planet that broadcast the love frequency.

Because you watch TV, your main imprinting comes through this mind-control machine, which imprints you basically with fear.

When you go through evolutionary processes, there is disorientation, chaos, confusion, and a lack of identity.

Humans are creatures of energy, and your emotions create a collective force that broadcasts chaos and fear but also anger. The anger is about what you are being denied down inside. It creates a stirring and mirroring of the planet's anger from the lack of care and the lack of love.

You are now pushed as people to your limits. The planet is also pushed. The solar plexus area is where you hold power in your body and where you extend your power out to the world. Imagination is the key to brilliance, to unifying conceptualizations, and to bringing ideas into realization.

Chapter 35
Sound Began The Whole Thing

In the beginning, there was sound. The sound began the whole thing, and in sound resides tremendous power. It opens doorways to other realities, for with the production of sound, an energy can move from one system to another. When you utilize sound, it is quite easy to bypass the logical mind, shifting the channel by intending and being clear.

The development of the re-bundled DNA expresses itself beyond logic through sound. Sound allows matter, as information that is formulating itself into the body, to find a proclamation of knowing outside the body.

You can move into a state of bliss when you surrender to expressing sound. To various degrees, that bliss is based on the feeling and knowing that you are not limited and that you exist as unbounded beings of light.

At the Institute, we use a powerful custom sound system, sound frequencies, and sound vibration of light language to help people in many ways.

We use it to reconnect, balance the body and the brain, de-stress, relax, and get rid of anxiety, helping clients find their purpose in life and recover their mastery.

All forms of life have these energy portals as doorways and places where they can be refueled. What each form of life does with its refueling is within the blueprint or the DNA of the form of life itself. As your DNA is being reordered into a new form of life, the frequency or identity that you carry is speaking to something on a nonphysical level. Life extension and rejuvenation of cellular life is part of building the light body, a body that is not so dense so that it does not self-destruct, a body that self-generates and self-replenishes.

That has attracted the attention of the Illuminades, the New World Order, and other government officials who were scared of the powerful energy that we use for healing frequencies.

So, one day we entered the office. The door was not broken, was still locked, and there were no signs of any breaking and entry, but our sound system had been vandalized and the inside of the office had been destroyed.

We could not file a report and go into detail about this event.

We do not believe in law enforcement, as corruption is everywhere.

They arrested a black woman who did not give a signal when she changed lanes. The police decided to pull her over and take her out of her car. They arrested her and took her to jail. Ironically, there is missing time on the video of her arrest. Then she was found in her cell hanging dead.

The point is that I, CHADD, am afraid of law enforcement in Florida because of police brutality and because I have been dropped on my head and handcuffed, though I can't stand up when I can't hold on to anything as I am confined to a wheelchair. There are over 3000 people who die each month from psychotropic drugs. When you say that you have insurance, within five minutes you are given a prescription for psychotropic drugs. How can you be properly diagnosed within five minutes? They pass out psychotropic drugs like candy.

Fifty years ago, people relied on family and friends to pull through things that happened in life like divorce, and bankruptcy... Back then you would have talked your way through this issue and certainly not have been medicated. These psychologists have been on the fringe of medicine for years. They wanted to be viewed as physicians. And it has to be a disease. They meet together, they vote, and they create a disease and a name for it.

Today they use a diagnostic book, a manual based on consensus, a very dangerous book. It contains many disorders that can apply to any one of us because the disorders are not real medical diseases.

And the damage has been done.

The doctors have created all these psychological deceptions and planted all these problems in Americans' minds. For instance, you can't watch TV for one hour without being bombarded by advertisements that claim that you are sick with bipolar or ADHA so on and so forth. Sicknesses have been implanted in Americans' minds subliminally.

If people let the government decide what foods they eat and what medicine they take into their bodies, they will be soon as sorry as souls that live under tyranny.

Therefore, refuse to bend and obey what is leading you to a certain death. Who are they to kill you?

Mom, it means that you are guilty in God's eyes, and you will be punished by God.

The government is out of control and manages to dictate our health destruction through the FDA and prescription drugs. One hundred thousand Americans die each year from prescription drugs.

This morning CHADD woke up with many Angels standing all over his bed. He got off his bed and reached for his breakfast. With the blueberry waffles ingested, he fell right away into a trance and found himself in the company of Mother Mary. She was standing in front of him. He lost totally track of time, enlightened by her radiance. So, we slept for a few hours together, as the God Duo, and went to have a bite to eat. Ran into one of Five Angels in a local eatery. And this beautiful Angel with white hair entered and stopped at VIE's level.

"Did we meet somewhere? It seems that I know you," she said.

VIE replied, smiling: "Maybe we know each other in another realm."

The Angel smiled back and then said to her "I guess that you have a look alike" Then she moved away from the table to the opposite side table.

We finished eating, paid and then drove toward the office. The rain began to pour, followed by lightning strikes and thunderstorms.

We were now out of the car and CHADD's arm was attacked by some entities. His arm was all red. VIE rapidly put her light on the area to clean him from this attack. The light was very soothing, and the redness slowly disappeared.

God was now talking to CHADD. He said: "Back your files, up both of you, on your two computers; one may be struck by the lightning." Then He added: "Never try to contact or see your family anymore."

Chapter 36
Archangels of Justice

Then we encountered the Archangels of Justice. Their mission is to uncover corruption within the criminal justice system and expose it to the public. They have a message for you:

"For a great many years, we have watched the criminal justice system crumble before our eyes. There are good police officers who need our help to rid their agencies of the bad. The only way for that to happen is for the citizens to take control of the internal affairs investigations. No longer allow police agencies to investigate their own."

Their mission is to uncover corruption within the criminal justice system and expose it to the public.

Doctors these days have a degree to write you a prescription for drugs; that's it. They diagnose you with anything in five minutes and write you a prescription for drugs that have been proven to have never cured anything; rather they unbalance your body and make you need more prescriptions for more drugs because of the side effects that they cause, and it goes on and on.

Then they prescribe you some blood tests, X-rays, and sonographs and even if you have insurance, you have to pay the deductible and more. It is a scam and all about money.

Doctors have long lost and forgotten the Hippocratic oath they took. They have gone beyond the limits of good tests, and medicine has become more of a business. It's about money and self-gain to the detriment of the health of the people.

It is no longer about helping people. We, CHADD & VIE, only respect doctors who work for the hospice of the comforter. Tri-county and

Associates are affiliated with the Illuminati. For instance, the doctors nurses, and practitioners who write the prescriptions go on vacation to the Bahamas, Hawaii, or anywhere in the world.

And then they do not dare to go to the funerals of their patients who have passed. How do you think our Father thinks about this?

Chapter 37
Eternal Life Exist Where Eternal Love Exist

Metatron said," A new meridian of time will come, and the foundations of the Earth will be shifted to a new magnetic foundation as the orbit of the Earth is reset within the ocean of Light. Those who seek spiritual freedom and autonomy from the structures of power will build communities of Love and Light throughout the world. They will use their soul and muscle to fashion healing centers of "Light" and teaching centers where the "Love" of God prepares the young to use the spiritual gifts of creativity. Eternal Life exists where eternal love exists.

Metatron here is announcing the arrival of Commandant Ashar Sheran.

According to Metatron, large biosatellites up to fifty miles in length and twelve in diameter will come to our planet. They will house the millions of emigrants that will proceed to other physical planets. Their amenities include crystallized environments that can change the atmosphere to suit the needs of the physical occupants.

Some biosatellites contain whole living environments that will take the place of the planetary environments that the occupants are being removed from.

The physical biosatellites used a specialized field of magneto-hydrodynamics to move them into a "geosynchronous" orbit within a given solar system. Here multiple planets can be attended to and instructed simultaneously by biosatellites. By modulating multiple radiation belts in direct south poles on the biosatellite, a special orbital vibration is created, which is used to maintain the biosatellite's operations concerning the planet.

Covering the exterior of the vehicle are bio-organisms, which make continuous repairs to the exterior and provide for thermal changes while going through the energy envelopes of different star systems.

Special planets with no radiation fields are selected for metallurgy and mining special minerals for motherships that are constructed out of the pattern of concentric atoms that can withstand maximum spectral irradiation.

Abundant food is created by reprocessing various soil nutrients through a changing light environment, which produces whatever food is necessary for physical survival. Through a blue-green light conversion process, the plant phase is bypassed, and the food staple is created immediately. Here a soil-like nutrient is mixed with seeds to rapidly produce whatever organic substance is necessary. In addition, this soil-like nutrient can be continuously used over and over again for other food items.

However, higher evolutionary races live off of light, which they synthesize for their energy supply. It is pulsated into them from a regenerating light environment.

Chapter 38
VIE uses the Language of the Light for Instant Communication

VIE speaks the language of the Light. She also tones, sings, and hand signs while CHADD is an Energy Retracting Transducer of God.

The language of the Light is instant communication with the Infinite Mind using ideographic and pictographic cybernetics.

It is used by the Elohim in conjunction with the Eternal Light. It is the parent of the language of Deity used in an overall plan or design to outline a procedure, code knowledge into the crystal, etc. The language of Light reaches many planetary words and reality levels simultaneously and fuses the different languages into the same scenario abstract.

This allows man to communicate with other planets of intelligence through super-holographic processes. As God's word. The knowledge of this language comes from a core memory of information being shared by the higher spiritual levels of existence. It allows man to read the "records of the mysteries" in the higher heavens.

And CHADD, being an Energy Retracting Transducer of God, is a speaker for the Lord Jesus- Christ. New verses come to CHADD randomly. He always has something positive to speak of.

That is why self-elected keep depriving him of rights and freedom. But "Beware of the doG."

Chapter 39
The Tainting of the Food All Over the World

An expert kept warning the Green Protection Agency that one day a disastrous chemical could spill into an important river in the country. And it finally happened. Tons of toxic water tainted with lead, arsenic, and other heavy metals poured into the Animas River when a contractor working for the Green Protection Agency inadvertently breached a Gold King Mine.

Following the breach, the contaminated water spread downstream into various other states. Initially, the Green Protection Agency said only about one million gallons of contaminated water, which turned the river yellow-orange, flowed into the river, but later the agency was forced to admit that the amount was close to three million gallons.

It appears as a possible set-up to justify a hidden agenda for the construction of a treatment plan and in the meantime the farmers get the poisoned food and then sell it to other countries. The Food and Drug Administration will let it pass to other countries. They will poison the entire world before the election. It may take five to ten years before it kills people, but it will poison then kill them. It is all money-making.

Chapter 40
A Flash Back inside an asylum: Fire in the Sky

This movie was about Travis Wilson. He was abducted by Aliens in the sky with fire.

He was working in the woods with my crew. There was a light down the road, and when he noticed the light coming through the trees, he wondered what that was. The light was coming from higher up, then down among the trees. As soon as they were at the place where the light was coming from, they saw a metallic object 100 feet away. Metallic in some areas and glowing in other parts, some light glass with lights glowing and a kind of rumbling sound. Then it started moving, and Travis started to jump to hide behind a log. Numbness came over him, then he blacked out. He was hit, and the hit instantly transported him inside the UFO. The crew started to yell at Travis to come back next to the truck. The crew was afraid when Travis vanished, then left to go back to town to make a report of Travis's disappearance.

Travis awoke with something covering his body. He had problems breathing, and pain in his head and chest, and saw some faces that did not look like the doctors he thought they were when he awoke inside. He had pain and trouble breathing in the small room, humid with these faces. When he turned around to get away from the table, they came close to them. They extended their hands towards him; their eyes were terrifying. Very disturbing eyes staring at him with a negative look. He tried to find a way out and came to a door. It was a room that was probably close to another. The chairs had some controls on them, and he tried to open a door to get out. Then he saw a man standing at the door. He thought that it was some man from NASA and talked to the man without getting an answer. The man took him outside of the UFO. He tried to look around, but the man seemed to be in a hurry. He could feel the air. There was some other UFO, and he tried to talk to other people. They got him on a table, and they put a mask on his face. Then he blacked out. Then he was feeling cold air; he was lying face down on the soil. He saw a slivery, glowing silent object disappearing in the air, fading away very fast.

He called his family, then his brothers-in-law. They saw it as a joke and hung up on him, thinking it was not funny. Then he called again, and his brother came to pick him up.

Thereafter, Travis went through a lot as the system tried to cover up. He went under investigation and had psychiatric tests and drug treatment as they said that he was hallucinating. It came out later that there had been a dramatic change in the trees where it happened.

There were many attempts to cover up. A guy with a badge, very intimidating, went to see him, left angry, then went to see the sheriff, and asked for a copy of the file. But he never got it; in the days after the event, the file had disappeared. Someone else from the military who was out to discredit the case went through polygraph tests and flunked them. Some Federal agents that also tried to intimidate did the same. Some parts disappeared from his book. Travis passed five polygraph tests.

The government used this man inside a facility to entrap people who had seen the movie.

CHADD looked at the wall inside the asylum. Travis's name was painted on the wall. CHADD recalled that many years ago he was in an HBO movie.

On the asylum wall was painted a big library with books on the shelves. His book was on one of the shelves.

Travis Wilson was abducted by aliens disappeared for five days and returned. He recovered consciousness while lying on his bed. He remembered huge eyes looking at him. Looking straight inside him. This creature did not look like anything he had ever seen. He started asking questions, and he saw through the door that the hallway was blue. Who are you people? Travis asked. He said that he did not do anything special to have this kind of experience. It can happen to anyone.

Psychiatric facilities have made big business out of it. Patients recognize and remember the movie made about the life of Travis Wilson. They read his name and start talking about it. This is all it takes from these Thuggees. They administer psychotropic drugs to the patients. The Thuggee doctors who were introduced into the United States are the ones who handle all the psychiatric places. They come from India and Pakistan and wear white blouses. They act like physicians and take everything out of context, then patients are trapped with no rights inside the asylum with drugs. Next step, they manipulate the brains of patients and record movies. Brainwash them and use the inmates' brains to create their reality. This is when they make it. A lot of patients die before being released. This is also part of the reduction of the population by the Third World Order.

The Savior affirms that beyond this lower system is a second underworld zone known as the "outer darkness" where the fallen demi-gods dwell, working to connect our consciousness operations with those of the greater zones of darkness. These fallen gods have great jurisdiction over all souls, but more so over souls who desire not to be responsible with their gift of Life.

Souls who do not work to evolve a greater Light consciousness give themselves over to dragon power or draconic entropy. They lose their soul-positioning power and, in many cases, their ability to continue the evolutionary process, falling from the potential orderings of light into the chaotic conditions of the substrata of creation.

When anyone is admitted into one of these places, even admitted, the door closes once they pass the front desk. People are trapped, and they are admitted also. Patients do not have any more rights and have to behave and do what they are told. They are told that if they do not take their medications, they will never see the outside again.

Beyond the Underworld are the realms of the chastisement of chaos, and even beyond those, there are the chastisements of the archons who are on the way to the midst.

Some are allergic to the medications but have to keep ingesting it. If they don't, they will be tied to a bed and given a shot. Some patients are forced to take up to 11 psychotropic drugs a day. Some have seizures, foam at the mouth, and vomit. Some are so overmedicated that they laugh all the time and do not even remember their name or the family phone number. It's all about money. To make a phone call you have to buy some phone cards. There are "cantinas" with no healthy choice of food, and it all costs two or three times what it costs outside. Patients are told when to pee, when to eat, when to talk, when to sleep, and when not to.

And at times some people are forced to go into their rooms. They are violently dragged to their room. Some have heart attacks with triple doses of drugs. No one is ever sent to an emergency room; the dead are buried with a cover story. Some violent murders are happening inside these places, and no one cares. And when CHADD descended, he lost his power and became without light, and no one helped him. And in his distress, he sang praises to the light and was delivered from his distress. And further, it freed his bonds and brought him up out of the darkness

and the oppression of chaos.

And he will thank the Light, for it delivered him, and its wondrous works have been given to the generation of Humankind.

And the Light has broken the upper gates. It caused him to leave the region where he had trespassed, and his power was taken away because he had transgressed.

He had abandoned its mysteries to the gates of chaos.

And when he was in distress, he sang praises to the Light and it saved him out of its oppressions.

The singing of praises to the Light, the calling out to the Light to break through the gates of the lower vibration, the gates of Heaven, freed him.

These gates are opened with special sounds, musical overtones, and heartfelt petitions.

Until then, the body of humankind is largely kept dysfunctional by not being focused enough on the Light energy to support the evolutionary process of the ascension.

Music is an incredibly powerful learning tool, particularly in infancy, when the ear out-performs the eyes in connecting with pre-birth memory, and intelligence is routed according to musical rhythms and pre-verbal cues.

Faith Wisdom, the Light, is now introduced. She closely resembles to the Queen of Sabbath; in that she is connected with opening the veils for higher worship. She is destined to become one with the Queen of the Heavens (the heavenly Church of the elect) through the Virgin matrix. There is a higher Mystery connected with the Virgin of Light.

Suddenly, at the end of time, a group of Divine souls will make their presence known on this planet.

Their arrival will not be predicted by the twelve constellations of astrophysical movement because they have no part of the system.

They travel in their spiritual dimensions amidst their Light pulsation. In addition, the model of the divine tetrahedron will be seen over various parts of the world.

And this will be the central control or administrating force of light, which will align new movements.

We have been confined to matter-energy light physics, and even the historical input of the Prophets and Jesus, which has for such a long time been circumscribed to a singular planetary understanding, will soon reveal itself as being Eternal.

When this is fulfilled, we will see how the Limitless Ones will allow boundaries to be opened so that those who have been in the open spaces can come to their true fulfillment by quickening themselves into new forms.

The soul should take precedence over the state of karma of the body. It is the soul that guides the body and chooses the direction it will take along the path.

This is where Free Will comes into play, for the soul may choose the power either of the Light or of the counterfeiting spirit.

The counterfeiting spirit is the spirit within each physical form as the vehicle that pretends it is of the Truth and of the Christ to entrap souls in chaos and pathways whereby, they cannot find their way to their true identity in the true Light. It is a consciousness of the lower rulers to overpower and control soul evolution.

Why is the small, innocent child brutally killed? It is the power of the Moira (destiny) created by the archons that connects the soul-only activity with the activities of this local life.

FREE WILL is the eleventh commandment. "No one should be deprived of Free will and Freedom."

The Juridical system deprives people of free will when they are court-ordering people into medications and chemotherapy.

It is known that the person who receives chemotherapy is going to die in terrible pain.

The thuggee doctors are depriving people of their free will when they force them against their will to ingest drugs, all with the approval of the judicial system.

Pharmaceutical companies are depriving people of their free will when they use physicians to keep people on drugs and reinforce vaccination shots in children when we know that they contain mercury poisoning.

Chapter 41
One of the Greatest World Crimes in History
"Kali or Bhavai"

We are among a tribe in the desert of Australia. We are surrounded by the Australian aborigines. They play the didgeridoo, and we are told that the chief is going to talk to us. He has very important news to tell us. The chief of the tribe, whose name is Wazizi, is making a sign to let them know that he is going to talk now.

"I called for you to come because I have very serious news to pass on to you. Thugs are a horrible tribe by the name of Bhavani. They worship Kali and sacrifice human beings to this goddess."

Kali is the wife of the Indian god Shiva. She is the Hindu goddess of destruction and death. She is known as a deity of war to the thugs. She is a black-skinned goddess with three glaring eyes, many arms, an open mouth displaying long teeth, blood-soaked lips, and an extended tongue coated with human gore. Only when appearing alone does Kali transform her true and hideous nature. The goddess through her gurus encouraged her earliest apostles to go forth and destroy unbelievers.

With each murder, the killer thug would attain a higher status in the hereafter. Moreover, the goddess was obligingly protective of her killers, disposing of the bodies of their victims so they could go on undetected.

An apprentice thug, unable to control his authority, though it is forbidden according to their tradition to cast eyes upon the goddess, turned to see Kali eating the body.

Ironically, the eternal rifts between Muslims and Hindus were put aside in that both religious sects joined the thugs, worshiping a Hindu goddess and putting her before all other gods.

Even stranger was the fact that before its wholesale eradication by the British, the sect was predominately Muslim, with followers risking everything to pay homage to this ancient Hindu image.

There is more to it.

We can all be murdered. The Third World Order is on its way with China and another part of the world.

Chapter 42
A bunch of Tyrants

CHADD and VIE are now transported to an Australian tribe. They are called for a tribe meeting by Chief Wazizi who needs to pass on some very important news regarding Planet Earth.

We are those who remain of the few who still carry the knowledge. Our ancestors still talk to us. We have been mass murdered and parked in the desert because of that. But we still remember how to travel, communicate with our ancestors, and carry the predictions of the future.

Our chief Wazizi has asked for you. You are the chosen one, and he needs to communicate some very important news regarding the American land. He will speak to you now.

Wazizi: I am passing along to you this message.

You must let American citizens be aware that anonymous martial law is in the US in a world run by unbelievably sick people. The biggest threat to the American country is the government that is telling the American citizens what to eat, breathe, sleep, and pray.

It's all about control of money. This is definitively going on US soil. It is a government conspiracy to eliminate the entire population. They capitalize on each death.

No one is immune based on color, age, creed, or religion. They indoctrinate people with sex, drugs, violence, FCC, porn. Politicians are in place to give the impression that people have freedom of choice. The illusion of the meaning of choice.

They continue to fight pointless wars because of congressional lies to ensure that the Federal Reserve propels the future of America's new generation of slaves and unborn children.

The government plan is to steal 17 trillion dollars from unborn American children. It is not a matter of if but when because the economy will collapse very soon. They are presenting lies to the American people.

If the government takes their right to carry guns as Americans, they are taking their right to defend themselves and their freedom.

Do not give up your rights.

The old man said that he could read the mind of anyone who did his homework correctly and tried to inform the population. This man wrote that the United States is the top producer of pornographic DVDs and web material. The second largest is Germany; they each produce more than four hundred porn films for DVD every week.

Pornography has moved from the margins of society into the very mainstream of American culture. From Internet pornography to MTV, pop culture industries bombard us with sexualized images of idealized women and hyper-masculine men that jump off the screen and into our lives, shaping our gender identities, our body image, and especially human beings' intimate relationships.

The dominant images and stories disseminated by the multi-billion-dollar pornography industry produce and reproduce a gender system that undermines equality and encourages violence against women. It is a mass-produced vision of sex that is profoundly sexist and destructive. A vision that limits the ability to create authentic, equal relationships free of violence and degradation.

In reality, the porn industry makes more money than Hollywood. Around thirteen thousand adult videos are produced annually, amassing over thirteen billion dollars in profit. Hollywood released five hundred movies and made only eight billion eight.

They also made more than The National Football League, The National Basketball Association, and Major League Basketball combined, and more than NBC, CBS, and ABC combined. In addition, nine years ago they already had larger revenues than the top technology companies (Microsoft, Google, Amazon, eBay, Yahoo, Apple, and Netflix combined).

Porn industry leaders have also said condoms were bad for business, leading to a decline in pornography sales. Several porn stars tested positive for HIV. But the porn industry is just a big industry; their main concern is money. Some porn actors with HIV and some aging in the industry die mysteriously.

All this is true, but there is more to say.

How do you deprive a nation of independent citizens of their freedom and turn them into slaves, and how do you do this slowly and imperceptibly, without violence, and with the willing participation of the slaves-to-be?

It is very simple, says Wazizi. While they are kept sleeping with chemtrails, and psychotropic drugs or burdened with their everyday life, trying to make a living and pay their bills, you bombard them with subliminal frequencies and messages; you corrupt them, undermine them, deprave them, and demoralize them until they have acquired all the characteristics of slaves.

Jews use pornography to destroy gentile morals. An academic Jewish society member said that though Jews make up only a very small percentage of the American population, they dominate the porn industry. Not only did he admit that Jews are the most successful pornographers, but he also celebrates the fact Jews have a grudge against Christianity.

In Rome, a few years ago, Italian, and Russian police, after working together, broke up a ring of Jewish gangsters involved in the industry of child rape and pornography. They had kidnapped non-Jewish children between the ages of 2 and 5 from an orphanage. Though AP and Reuters both ran stories on the episode, US media conglomerates refused to carry the story on television news, saying that it would prejudice Americans against Jews!

It is Human Time to allow a new vision. When the Creator exists and is welcomed as truth, false illusions, and perspectives cannot remain. This is occurring on the Earth now for a great percentage of humanity. While it is a process of moving towards experiences of love and bliss, the journey can awaken all the energies of challenge, suffering, insecurity, and fear from within the old consciousness of your being.

As the light is accepted, it goes into human consciousness, aura, body, and cells to discover any remaining darkness, so that it can be healed.

This "darkness" is comprised of "blocks" within beings that are afraid to change, afraid to transmute. Once people are aware of these blockages that have not yet been released, they can participate in their clearing. Once humans remember how to clear themselves, they can assist others with their clearing. The higher light arrives from the dimensions beyond time. Hence, it moves into human beings present, past, and in alternative realities.

In this way, the injuries that have been taken on throughout the myriad embodiments in a third-dimensional vessel can be healed from within. Fortunately, the antidote to the lies that have been told, the mistakes that humans have made, and the hardships they have endured is that they know that they can refuse to participate in any version of reality.

As humans begin to control their reality in this manner, they realize that they can transmute and release any experiences that they deem complete. They also remember that the antidote to any fear and or pain that re-emerges is to send Unconditional Love and Violet Fire to themselves.

It is the time to step out through the doorway of their heart so that they can witness themselves and let go of these old perceptions of themselves held by the ego mind. It is important to just witness how the ego mind has created restrictions through fear-based dialogue and self-criticism. All these projections from the ego have been undermining humans' ability to be free and to move forward into new realms of experience within themselves.

It is time to allow a new vision of themselves to emerge and begin to align with who they are at this moment. They can do this now so simply. With the new frequencies of light coming onto the planet, there are unlimited possibilities for each one to break out of their old boundaries, out of perceptions of limitation and lack. Now is the time for the sacred promise to be revealed through the light that can be accessed within the reflections of light from the sun.

It is humans' time for liberation and for their abundance to be restored to them. They must reach within their consciousness into the reflected light that holds the reconnection to the source.

It's through this powerful force of the sun's energy that they can be held. Humans must remember.

These reflections of light carry a natural fluidity within them, and that fluid light is weaving throughout the earth's plan at this time and creating a womb-like energy to be held around each one. This womb-like energy that surrounds all humans is supporting their rebirth. As they reach out to the light reflections of the sun with their consciousness, their cells take in nutritional aspects that are held within these reflected light rays.

Chapter 43
VIE's First Near-Death Experience

I tried to see something. There was a bright light at the end of a tunnel. The smell was suffocating me. I tried to reach my nose, but my arm would not move; then came this horrible taste in my mouth, it was brown and thick, like a thick brown cream coming from a tree seed crushed into a puree.

As my spirit slowly moved away, I could see it standing eight feet before me. My spirit was so perfect, dressed in a white gown, free flowing, just above my ankle. I was walking on the most beautiful beach.

The water was so clear that I could see every fish as if I were in an aquarium. There was no wind, and the sand was bright white and very fine. The water under my feet was warm. I was totally at peace.

Then I saw a brilliant light, and suddenly I was aware of the most beautiful garden I have ever seen surrounding the beach. That is when I began to hear celestial music very clearly and see vividly colored flowers. The music was so celestial it is hard to describe it.

In the background were beautiful mountains with many different hues. They appeared to be twenty miles away. My vision was so much clearer than before.

I saw people having a good time. Some were playing music, some were playing some weird instruments, some were singing and others toning.

Further away was a group of people seated on the grass in a circle. They seemed to be having an important reunion. Their faces were covered with paintings, like a mask. I could hear them talking but I could not understand what they were saying. Their language seemed familiar to my ears, but it was not a language that I could understand. They were drinking a beverage made from a root extract one by one, all from the same cup.

Then they stood up and still in a circle began a tribal dance chanting Piloo! Piloo! Piloo! Piloo! They wore some type of primitive costumes and were barefoot, beating the floor in cadence.

Finally, the oldest man came to me, walking very slowly with a face that had no expression. But very pleasantly and sweetly, though in a tone voice, announced:

"You are in the land of the ancestors. We lived on Earth, on the Caillou, just like you until we came here. Everything is kept in place by Master-Vibration, which prevents aging. It is tone like you sometimes when you give healing sessions to your clients.

"That is why everything looks so vivid and bright. Nothing wears out here. Everything over here is pure. The elements do not mix and break down like on planet Earth and the "Caillou." We live in peace and harmony with nature and God.

"There is no disease; disease is manmade. Cancer does not exist, and we do not take any vaccinations. We do not need them. They have been created by dark energies to kill you and keep only the strongest as their slaves.

You came here, to the land of the ancestors, because we have called you to receive that message. You must pass it to the people when you return. Tell them everything I am telling you and everything you have seen.

You have an important work to do on earth. Your mission is not finished. You must go back and finish it. But from now on we will keep in touch with you. You will hear from us.

You must write about what you saw and what we have told you. Go now and make sure you pass the message, and it will all end well! Ta ta!

I could feel a presence next to me, whose face I could not see. It was a masculine and reassuring presence. I felt it was very protective. I felt safe and was aware of the love coming from the center of his chest. It felt like bliss. Light rays also shone all around him. I wanted to stay because I felt so full of Joy and Love.

Then I heard his very soft voice saying, "VIE, we have more to accomplish, you and me.

"We also must write about the Black Aggie in DC. We must also sing about it. We must reach as many people as we can and awaken them before they are reduced to slavery. Also, we must try to save as many as we can from death. It is already written anyway, but the prophecy must be accomplished. Do not worry how it will happen; we just have to do it."

I then found myself being transported into a radiant beam of rainbow light that turned out to be the white light emanating from a circular opening far above me, and I was back to my body.

Chapter 44
VIE's second N.D.E.

Three years later I had another near-death experience. My heart stopped beating due to an overdose of antibiotics.

I was going through the same experience. I was in the tunnel and saw a bright light at the end. I saw my spirit still dressed in a white gown and observed myself.

I woke up very tired. I had to join CHADD in a battle while sleeping.

For twenty days, he'd been physically attacked. It began with his neck, then his feet were marked, and finally, his left arm was bleeding. This was enormous. He was exhausted, and I was exhausted too.

He was told that his mother did not want to let him go and had such a strong grip that she ripped his flesh very badly.

There was a woman named Aggie, a nurse working in a hospital. It seemed that patients under her care died at an unnatural rate. Suspicion grew; she was convicted of murder and put to death.

Some communal feelings of guilt spread, and a statue was put in Druid Ridge Cemetery in her honor.

When the statue was unveiled, strange occurrences started happening.

People have been found dead in front of the statue, including a pledge from a local fraternity. Pregnant women who walk in the figure's shadow (where, oddly, the grass never grew) suffer miscarriages. People began to gather at the graveyard at night, which became a frequent

problem. Then one morning, the necessary employees walked into work and found the statue of Black Aggie with only one arm. The other had been sawed off.

Eventually, the statue was removed from Druid Ride Cemetery and donated.

The statue is now displayed in DC.

The statue was a rather eerie figure by day, frozen in a moment of grief and terrible pain.

At night the figure was unbelievably creepy. The shroud over its head obscured the face. The statue's eyes' glowed red at the stroke of midnight, and any living person who returned the gaze would instantly be struck blind. If you sat on her lap at night, the statue would come to life and crush you to death in her dark embrace. If her name was spoken three times at midnight in front of a dark mirror, the evil Angel would appear and pull over you down to hell. It's also said that spirits of the dead would rise from their graves in the dark to gather around the statue at night.

The disruption caused by the statue grew so acute that it was donated to Washington, DC.

Now I see what will happen very shortly.

The original statue is today at the federal courts building in Washington, close to the White House. The statue has been placed there to kick out all the dark energies of people who elected themselves to these key places and took power and control of humanity. And nothing can stop it now.

Then the truth will be exposed.

The adversary plants weeds, teaching the pursuit of material things, money power, and prestige. His servants create, foster, and encourage narcissism, entitlement, rudeness, and dominant behavior.

We were bombarded by advertisements and thought that we had to suffer this propaganda to enjoy our lives. We were also taught to believe that they were indestructible and to accept their unchanging reality in our lives. Now all is changed.

Once humans will find out that the world, they have been taught to believe in by the media is fake, it will be transformed.

Highly advanced souls can transform themselves into a different state without having to undergo physical death.

The human beings on Earth that are ready now have access to the Elixir of Immortality that has been guarded all along, as well as advanced technology that will heal our planet.

But to ascend each one has the choice to focus on the positive and avoid re-creating the cycles of torture and pain that have plagued us for so long. Each one must learn to be more loving, accepting, and forgiving of each other. Each must realize that we are all one and learn humility, patience, kindness, and regardless of who they may be, support the goodness of others without judging.

The further you go in this direction, the more likely you are to transform into the next level of evolution and ascend.

I am hearing words spoken by the person that I already felt, the male presence next to me, whose face I never saw.

"This is the Key. VIE, let them know that this is the Key to ascend."

Chapter 45
Revelation 13

What is the Seven-Headed Wild Beast of Revelation Chapter 13?

The wild beast with seven heads introduced in Revelation 13:1 represents the worldwide political system.

It has authority, power, and a throne, which points to its being a political entity, in Revelation 13:2.

It rules over "every tribe and people, and tongue and nation," so it is greater than a single national government.

It combines features of the four beasts described in the prophecy of Daniel 7, including the appearance of a leopard, the feet of a bear, a lion's mouth, and ten horns.

The beasts in Daniel's prophecy are identified as specific kings, or political kingdoms, that rule succession over empires, in Daniel 7:23. Thus, the wild beast of Revelation 13 represents a composite political organization.

It ascends:" Then I saw a Beast coming out of the sea" – that is, from the turbulent masses of mankind that are the source of human governments. (Revelation 13:1; Isaiah 17:12-13)

The Bible says, "And that no man might buy or sell, save he that had the mark, or the name of the beast, or the number of his name." (Revelation 13:17-18) That expression indicates that the beast is a human entity, not a spirit or demon entity.

Even though nations may agree on a few things, they unite in their determination to maintain their

authority rather than submit to the rule of God's Kingdom. (Psalm 2:2)

They will also join forces to battle God's armies commanded by Jesus Christ at Armageddon, but this war will result in the nations being destroyed. (Revelation 16:14, 16:19:19-20)

"Ten horns and seven heads." Certain numbers are used symbolically in the Bible. Ten and seven, for example, represent completeness. The key to understanding the specific meaning of the "ten horns and seven heads" is an "image of the wild beast" identified later in Revelation 13:14, 15:17:3.

The Bible says that the seven heads of this red beast mean "seven kings" or governments. (Revelation 17)

Likewise, the seven heads of the beast of Revelation 13:1 represent seven governments: the primary political powers that have dominated through history and have taken the lead in oppressing God's people.

Chapter 46
Poltergeist

A creepy curse dogged the trilogy of films Poltergeist I, Poltergeist II, and Poltergeist III and their casts. Five cast members died in unexpected circumstances in the three years following the film production.

The poltergeist uses physical disturbances around certain people, usually children. Nasty habits include upending tables, chucking pots, banging in the wall, starting fires, and goofing around with electromagnetic fields. Curse, noise, knock, rattle— demons.

The poltergeist controls everything in a very disturbing matter, and your soul has to fight constantly.

Tesla positive, negative resistance. Pros and cons.

The positive is Jesus Christ, and the negative is demonic possessions.

When you have an item that is possessed by the devil, your life is in shambles, and you don't even know why.

There is a way out of that horrible lifestyle. A way to be free from sin and out of the dark environment that envelops you when you are possessed by the devil, and you don't even know it. Do it before it's too late.

It is to pray that prayer" I accept Jesus Christ as my Lord and Savior." When you speak these words out loud, the demons tremble with fear.

There is a better way. Get baptized and you will be on the path to righteousness.

Love, hate make your choice. You will be a different spirit then and in peace.

Because you will never understand until the end of time why your life is in shambles. Your spirit is not your own. Salah! (Pause and think about it.

Chapter 47

An Unfolding Saga

We are moving through the storm very quickly before the calm. Today, changes are being accelerated by human beings in the global transformation. Major changes are intense to the point of becoming chaotic.

In physics, chaos is a temporary phase between one natural state of harmony and its transformation into a higher form. The transformation phase between the two states becomes very stormy until the higher form is reached.

New colors of the fifth dimension are now being shown to us in the sky. Humans are absorbing these new colors, and they are activating brains and some DNA. It is activating brains and DNA and entire bodies and beings.

The five higher rays have been brought to you to cleanse and clear and bring forth the balance and harmony that you desire. The fifth higher rays have been brought forth to give you even greater assistance, as you integrate the love of your sacred heart.

We see evidence in ancient texts as well as architecture and art that we have had intergalactic help to shape human history, culture, civilization, and technology. Ashtar Sharan plays a significant role in Earth's Ascension today.

Although there have been many resources used to hide the evidence from our society, much is becoming apparent today.

Plato described Atlantis as a city that existed 9,000 years ago. According to ancient Greek texts, this city was established by an extraterrestrial called Poseidon. Poseidon was a Pleiadian whose father was Cronos and whose mother was Rhea.

In the Judeo-Christian tradition, we see Joshua bringing down the walls of Jericho by blowing a ram's horn. "In the beginning was the word, and the word was with God" (John 1:1.) This word of creation is OM. (A.U.M.) This is a program of Sound and Light that brings the etheric DNA program coding into the material world.

In Chinese astronomy, the constellation Capricornus is located in the black Tortoise of the North.

When we look at this history with modern eyes, we see that when the extraterrestrials were chumming the sea, they were accessing the DNA from the star- seeds from the sea part of the sky, from the galactic center, and they used a mandala or mandala, which is coded divine blueprint and mount, known today as a way to stream software programs or mount file systems. In other words, the DNA from the extraterrestrials was being cut into the DNA of the humans to form a new divine blueprint, which has been referred to as the Adam Kadmon. All humans are descendants of the galactic human hybrid on Earth.

A similar story is told in Greek, Hindu, and Chinese astrology literature. During the first Earth creation, after losing their immortality and Kingdom, men of Earth approached the Elohim Angels, who are the Angels who never fell, who have been guiding and guarding those on Earth from the dark ones, the fallen Angels.

Indeed, Ashtar wrote one of the Puranas. Commandant Ashtar explains in this literature how to live the life of a Bodhisattva on Earth and advises on all areas of living, including education, culture, medicine, weaponry, and star travel. Ashtar's one Earth incarnation was as Pascal Votan in the Mayan culture. He wrote the written record of Mayan mythology called the Popol Vuh. Tahtzibichen, a labyrinth archaeological site, is thought to be an entry into the mystic underworld. Xibalba. Truly it is modeled after the descriptions in the Popol Vuh and was built after that era.

The original Lords of the Dead existed in a realm, not on Earth.

This part of the Popol Vuh is recounting the Orion War.

Earth was colonized after the Orion War by those who survived. In the Chilam Balam book of the jaguar priests it is written: "A road to the stars descended from the sky and the 1 and 9 Gods came to Earth."

The 13 and 9 Gods refer to the Gods of the extraterrestrials of the Galactic Federation who will return to Earth when the Mayan calendar enters the unity wave of consciousness and counts natural time as 13 and 9 instead of 13 and 20. We entered the unity wave on March 9, 2011.

There is a direct reference to the same extraterrestrials who arrived from outer space to colonize Earth. The Xibalta Lords were the fallen Angels who tortured the slave races of Earth and created the destruction of Earth by nuclear holocaust.

Inter-dimensionally and multi-dimensionally, our radiant Planet is now ascended. As the cabal falls, they will no longer strip the Earth of her vital life force diamonds, gold, platinum copper, iron, coal, minerals, and trace minerals.

There is a place in Siberia where there are a dozen coal mines in one town. It is not only coal being mined. Siberia is populated by falsely accused prisoners. They are tortured and mine Mother Earth of precious minerals. There is no contact with the outside world. No one in the past 100 years has witnessed the vast destruction here.

This is taking us to Africa, to wars, killing, and the raping of women and children. The purpose is to make refugees flee from areas heavily populated with precious minerals. Genocide leaves no one to witness the rape of the Earth's gold, diamonds, platinum, and minerals for the production of computers as well as uranium for nuclear weapons.

But all is finished now. All is over thanks to Ashtar Sheran and his wings dissolving all equipment and structures associated with these places. With the arrests around the corner, these places will no longer exist. The destruction to the people and the planet will no longer exist. All resources will be fairly distributed to all people over the planet. This will happen with new harmless technologies.

We see giant networks of satellites connected to a computer system that is involved with making weather, including destructive storms. The entire system has been dissolved by Ashtar Sheran.

We see work on opening Mother Earth's portal to other stars. Much traffic from StarCraft entering and exiting from a portal running from the Amazon jungle to Hawaii.

Lady Nada enters the Amazon portal inter-dimensionally to restore another Solar Disc and anchor it into this era. This means Mother Earth can now govern itself with no one group or government interfering. We now go together with Zarathustra and Neptune, with sea beings, Angels, and Galactic in ships, and with the Cetacean Nation into the sea.

Ashtar dissolves all structures built and installed under the sea.

War weaponry, sonar, infrared, explorations, mass harvest of sea life, fishing vessels, cruise ships, submarines, barges with medical waste, barges with trash will no longer be allowed. With the controlling families and greed crumbling, these entities are dissolved.

This is the end of time on Earth for the duality school of Karma. Earth is ascending into a realm where we return to an enduring peace. We return to our full capacities as a Galactic Society.

At this time, all beings on this planet are facing themselves and the choices they have made. They are being invited to examine their positions and their goals. Anyone who does not honor a path of unity, openness, accountability, truth, and peace will soon, very soon, find that they have chosen a dead-end path.

That moment is fast approaching, and the rip and the gap between directions is widening every second. A separation of the paths is upon people now. We call this the separation of worlds. No longer will deceit and domination of others prevail.

You will see the evidence in the coming days. 9/11 revelations compelling war crimes trials are already rising to the top of the list, which involves most players in the past administration and quite a large number that remain in the current administration. Indictments will shortly be released on most of these, and others will follow.

These are convicting themselves and revealing their agendas every moment now.

Approximately 400 members of Congress are so corrupt that they have already been replaced by solid holograms. When their indictments are revealed, the holograms will be de-powered by the King of Swords.

Ones not ready or spiritually prepared to do the ascension clearing going on in 3-D levels will be sent to what appears to be a continuation of things as they now exist on a mirror image of old Earth and will not be coming to New Earth. This will be an Earth parallel in another dimension.

There will be announcements and the enactment of NESARA Law. Millions of starships from the Galactic Federation will decloak over all the major cities of the planet so that no one can say that they do not believe that they are here, or that they don't exist. The spontaneous reaction to massive decloaking will deeply affect consciousness in a single simultaneous event, everywhere, and absolutely will expose the cover-up of the galactic presence.

Chapter 48
Ashtar Sheran

"This thy country shall be saved as by miracle! I say not it will be peaceful deliverance but through the unfaltering loyalty of millions who place their face in thy Master, the Christ of God. This land will be cleansed from the abominations now infesting it. It shall be the center from which shall issue those injunctions and powerful energies which shall lead the world into an intense, burning desire to know and to do the will of the Lord God of all creation, as revealed by their King, who shall reign over this regenerated world without hindrance from those who now harass and seek to destroy His faithful servants.

"As we have our announcement and landings, everyone will have full access to the records of their cosmic souls as well as those of all earth embodiments. When we dropped to the 12th dimension in this matter universe, we had to create a matter vehicle. All met in the Lyran-vegan system, and the Adam Kadmon template we all now inhabit is the result of our joint agreement in Lyra. Only the negative Anunnaki from Niburu refused to abide by the Lyran compact, and some are still here in their original format. We call them the Illuminati/ family of 13.

"They are Mother Sekhmet's children who must now either open to Love or leave, permanently. The positive Anunnaki are what we call intergalactic temporal time cops, who come back here to remove the negative ones who are intergalactic criminals, operating against the universal and spiritual laws.

The end of time for the intergalactic war criminals is upon us."

Chapter 49
A Most Troubling Dream

The vision began with a fight in court between a judge and the public defendant. Now I see another judge. The new judge is in a military uniform.

I sat down and while the attorney general claimed her authority, she made a troubling comment that she was just named for this case but knew nothing about it. Looking at the record on the computer screen, she said to the judge:

"Judge, why do you release a judgment and not follow up to apply your judgment on your case here? What are the laws for in this case if you do not see that they are applied, and the laws followed?

"Judge, I am asking that CHADD not get out of this building but go straight from here to jail."

She did not know the important omissions, the missing parts of the record, and what happened in the past year.

It was never recorded. Because that change was made without court hearings, and all was unlawfully done.

The judge a year ago decided to send the man of God to an asylum for 489 days followed by two months in a thuggee's mental hospital, then to another mental hospital, and finally to have him admitted to another state asylum. None of that was recorded, and the attorney general thought that he was running free.

Nothing was reported, of course, of the beatings, the injections to which he was allergic, the repeated poisoning of food and drink, the drugs dumped into a chemical solution before being given to him every day, the foods eaten by the rats before it was served, and more of the atrocities he went through. The withholding of liquids. Nor, of course, that he served twice for the same offense without any court hearing and that his attorney (public defender) was against him and never defended him.

So, the judge cut it short and reported to the audience one week later. "To be continued."

A few days later, VIE went to a bookstore and bumped into an English gentleman. He had in his hand a book that attracted VIE's attention. The vibration of the man attracted her too. VIE felt that she needed to talk to this man.

She passed her hand in front of him to pick up the same book on the shelf in front of him. The man looked at VIE and began to talk to her.

"I was in Desert Storm, and I have seen some terrible and very disturbing things. All that this book is saying is true."

You know I am Catholic, not fervent like these Islamic people, but you know He is my God and The God. That man, Jesus, was only full of love, he was teaching only love and he died on the cross teaching the truth about love.

"These Islamic do not even look human, and they are invading the world to reduce the population in slavery. I am buying this book, and everyone that can afford it should buy it and it should be passed on to as many as possible.

"They are invading everywhere and have also taken away the judicial system. They have been put in all key places. People must read about it."

I just read something so true; God will not hold us blameless. Silence in the face of evil is evil itself, and not to speak is to speak.

The Islamic did not expect the followers of Christ to remain so calm, so determined, and they can't understand why they have not broken their will.

And I awakened from the dream with this thought – there are no accidents. I was given that dream for a reason.

Chapter 50
Using the Thuggee Doctors to Baker Act

I am witnessing that about every two months, they repeat their act of mental manipulation and create the same scenario. They talk to him and try to make him marry and procreate with the wrong DNA. What is the purpose of it? Well, two good reasons at least. Its acts make him look insane and keep him in their control with no freedom. In doing that, the dark government hopes to install their New World Order, a reign of control over the human population.

The NWO sent a false prophet. He pretends to be sent to help humanity ascend to a higher dimension and will try to create a new Christian church all around the globe under his name before the return of Christ. Another way to control humanity and CHADD's money.

We went back to the parking lot of the church and on the way to turn on the left, passing by the entrance to the road of my family subdivision, I was really tired and trying to find a solution, so I grabbed the Holy Bible from the Divine Mercy Chapel and put it on his lap. The reaction was immediate. His whole body began to tremble, and again he was choked by invisible and demonic Spirits. From that moment on, it got worse.

CHADD had to trick the Devil. The Devil trusts everything he is hearing. He called me the anti-Christ and asked me to get away from him. Then he grabbed the steering wheel, and the car went in zigzags to finally stop just in front of an electrical post. Behind the post was a retaining pond where he said that he wished to drown me.

Weirdly, I saw in the rearview mirror that the firefighters were already there, some putting red cones in the middle of the street and others running towards the car to ask me if I wanted the sheriff to be called.

I quickly and calmly replied that I was on my way and close to the church to see a priest to pray for him and to bless him. I found a deacon who agreed to pray on him, but it did not much change the situation.

That night I could drive him back to his apartment, but I had to wait over two hours until he finally agreed to get out of the car. His feet were swollen and hurting him. (His toes are connected to the grounding and a sign of Pisces.) So, I massaged them to help the blood circulate. Then I helped him transfer from the car seat to his chair. I had to run to the driver's side to take my purse and the car key. By the time I came back to the other side, he was lying on his back on the concrete. He started again to tell me horrible words.

From the corner of my eyes, I saw the dark entity sending him telepathic commands. The clone was in a human form, but his eyes were fixed. The face had no expression, no emotions. It looked empty without a soul.

Many persons passing by offered to help him get back on his chair, and each time he rejected help and repeated the same horrible things about me.

Finally, at eleven PM, one black man came towards him and said you are still resting on the floor. I saw you on the floor like two hours ago. Let me help you. You cannot stay there. My brother works here as security and if he sees you, he will call the police. Suddenly, another man came out of the building walking towards him. I recognized the man who took the time to sit next to him on the concrete floor of the parking lot and listen to his story. And I realized that I saw the black man going toward the entrance of the building talking to someone on the phone. This was it; they were the observers. The ones sent to observe his behavior.

They picked him up, and the white man left while the black insisted on pushing his wheelchair to the room. The black man named Tito insisted on coming for five minutes inside the room, saying that he had something to say to CHADD. "I passed and saw you on the ground hours ago and it reminded me that I buried my daughter a week ago, and she was in the same circumstances that you are, but she did not have your luck. Nobody picked her up."

Suddenly in front of Tito, CHADD began to suffocate and was choked seriously again. He was attacked once more by an invisible spirit.

At the same time that he was battling and grabbing for air, he rolled his chair very quickly out of the place, followed by Tito. When I came to the lobby, CHADD rapidly took the door out, and Tito turned towards me, looking very upset, and said, "You seemed to be a very nice lady. Go to the room and try to get some rest. You seem to need it. He'll be okay now that he is back in his wheelchair. I will keep an eye on him." Thus was the pre-arrangement made for CHADD's third time in an asylum. To the state DKF.

When I woke up in the morning, I found CHADD in his wheelchair in the park. His shirt was gone, and he smelled horrible. His jeans were soaked with urine. I understood right away. This had always happened when he had to fight the dark and invisible spirits. He then noticed my presence and spit on me. I gave him the key to the room and left knowing that he had food and drink and hoping that leaving him alone would help him finally sleep. It was now five days that he had not slept.

Once again, the dark black government used the chip they had inserted while in the first asylum to manipulate his brain. Not only did they chip him, but they combined it with some kind of chemical substance that they put in his brain.

The following morning, I called him, and he picked up. "Where are you? I am weak from lack of sleep and need your help. I cannot manage alone; this place is dangerous." I helped him get in bed and left.

I called in the early morning on my way to bring him some breakfast but got no answer.

I opened the door, and I saw his wheelchair empty, his shoes on the floor, his wallet on his wheelchair opened, and his ID out. Then I looked at the bed and saw that his bag had been searched and his clothes were all upside down half out of the bag. I called his name and went to the bathroom. But CHADD was nowhere to be found.

I heard the cleaning woman in the hallway and went to ask her if she knew where he was.

"I heard that he was taken to a hospital. But that is all I know."

The short blond front desk girl arrived just at that moment and waved at me. "Is everything okay?" To which I replied, "No. Not really. My friend is nowhere to be found. His wheelchair is there, his shoes are there, but I can't find him."

Kimberley replied, "Oh my God! Let's see, let me find out what happened." This girl, I found out later, was one of them. All had been pre-arranged as an excuse to arrest him again.

He called 12 hours later and asked me to come and visit him. "I'll tell you everything."

At the door, I was asked for a security code that I did not have. It was a big double door, securely locked. "How would I know that I need a security code?" I spoke. "And how do I get one?"

"Take a seat and wait."

I took a seat and waited for about fifteen minutes, then I heard the door unlocking and a face appeared. "Come on in, actually I need to talk to you and ask you some questions."

It was clear that I was there to answer some questions but was not allowed to ask any unless I signed some papers. The first thing I heard was "He has been Baker Acted and we need you to sign some legal papers for us."

Wow! Who do they think they are, and who am I, here? They Baker Act my blue flame, admit it and tell me to shut up and sign. Let us see about that.

While one was showing me the papers, a second person showed up, and they began to talk. That's how I learned that they did not know how to handle the case legally. Someone needed to sign and become his guardian.

Then they brought him. He was in a hospital gown looking miserable. They brought him naked. He looked me straight in the eyes and said in a very strong voice," Do not sign anything." But the way around came very quickly when the blond woman said, "Your demand to be his guardian will have to be approved by the judge first thing the next morning, and you will need to be present. And the judge may or not approve. He may decide to keep him under the appointed proxy."

So, I thought, they wanted to use me to legalize their action and get out of their responsibilities. Fine, I think, let me sign, get all the information and the security code, and then cancel it by never appearing in front of the judge. And I did. That's when I found out that the supposed guardian was the unit's psychiatrist. He was in charge of the unit with the tri-regional doctors. The Thuggees.

And from here I learned how they were so useless and did not know how to handle him and his case, what to do to balance his brain and stabilize him. The blond woman, among a lot of irrelevant questions, asked me: "What do you do to balance him? What do you suggest that we do?"

Again, wow! They are asking me now! But they are the ones in power with their earthly inefficient degrees. They manipulate his brain with a combination of a chemical substance that they have put in his brain and a chip that has moved into his brain. And now they are scared of him. He spat on them and told them some revelation that he was aware of that they did not understand.

What happened is they had appointed many observers around him during the two months he'd been released from the second asylum. And they began to be scared when he fell in the parking lot cursing everyone. Though they were waiting for an opportunity to control him again.

Who do they think they are? Now they are caught in their infernal machine. And they have to deal with it.

So, I replied to the blond woman: "Give him a lot of fluids, a fresh bottle of water, and a lot of rest. Let him sleep as much as he needs and no drugs."

On the big screen TV behind her, I heard the latest news on CNN and the announcement of a shooting, and it reminded me of the following.

There are no "good guns." There are no "bad guns." Any gun in the hands of a bad man is a bad thing. Any gun in the hands of a decent person is no threat to anybody except bad people. Charlton Heston, born John Charles Carter.

And here it is Roseburg Oregon (CNN)

The gunman who opened fire at Oregon's Umpqua Community College singled out Christians, according to the father of a wounded student. The gunman entered the classroom firing. "I've been waiting to do this for years," he said. The gunman, while reloading his handgun, ordered the students to stand up and asked if they were Christians, the student told her family. "And they would stand up and he said, "Good, because you're a Christian, you're going to see God in just about one second."

And I heard myself thinking, "Just take a minute to think about it!"

Was this man mentally manipulated and used to do this horrible act of killing? Of course! Psychotropic drugs.

Chapter 51
VIE's thymus attack

At the same time that CHADD was Baker Acted and admitted to another psychiatric unit in a downtown hospital, VIE was fighting a spiritual battle through a physical attack.

The dark spirits have put a sort of plastic dome on her thymus bone, blocking the chi and restricting the flow of the chi through the neck and the brain.

VIE was in great pain. First, she did not quite understand what had happened, and for a good five days, she tried to heal her throat like she would have for a sore throat. By the sixth day, she realized that it was more spiritual than physical, and she began to work on it with her spiritual Holy Family and Angelic Guidance. By the end of the week, everything was back to normal.

Desperate to get her, finally they implanted aliens' candida. This fungus kept her bloated and with great pain in the belly at night, sweating and leaving her unrest in the mornings. Depleting the body of all nutrients but... "Beware of the doG- a destiny for..."

Chapter 52
Astara, Zemeea and Estene

As I write this, I feel the energies embracing me and lifting me to a much higher place.

The minute I learned what they had done to my blue flame I was furious. How dare they Baker Act him again!

I rapidly called upon the psychic surgeons to come to take care of the issues that corrupt and demonic psychiatric and physician "doctors" have created.

Three psychic surgeons from the beyond, unseen realm immediately responded to my call and introduced themselves

They go by the sound name:

Astara is the main one and will be working on the chip.

Zemeea is a psychic spiritual surgeon.

Estene is a female and will work on the damage caused by the chemical, the drugs...

They volunteered to deactivate the implanted chip, remove it, and repair the damage as no other way would be safe.

The surgery is done by two clouds. It's like a cloud from space moving through CHADD's body that can work while he is awake or asleep.

One cloud pulls out all clogged poison by absorbing it and removes all the damage done to organs, bones, cells, blood, and DNA.

The second cloud is a yellow/ white/ blue/ green color, follows the first cloud almost immediately, and repairs everything.

I do not know how long I was out of body, but suddenly I was catapulted back into normal consciousness.

Chapter 53

Free Will Choice Will Rule

I bathe in that energy brought down from the highest Divine source and feel it entering my head, tingling with the energy. Out of the corner of my eye, I can see Wavoka (the Messiah) looking at me as I bathe myself in this energy, and I feel myself floating upwards, cloaked in a beam of light.

I am getting the sense that all of this is about the journey. It is all about that journey that never ends! It is of no great consequences. It will achieve what has been set out to do and do so with a brave heart.

To find a balanced solution to any discord, first, you must let go and let God! No levels of personality can be included in the seeking of truth, no ego or any thoughts that support self-gain or self-aggrandizement can be present during such a Heavenly desire. Intentions must be the purest and only ever intended for the greatest good of all concerned. They are Laws of Creation that must be adhered to beyond all else. Divine love is the guarantee of success.

Laziness, aloofness, lethargy, and unconcern are no longer excuses. Everyone walks on his own feet, by her convictions. Once you let go and let God, God takes all the responsibilities and releases you from all burdens, conditions, pain, and suffering.

You must surrender and declare "Not my will be done, but Thy will through me as your instrument be done."

The God Duo are called upon now in this present age of chaos and demonstrations to show the man of

Earth how to release his moral will gift to the Higher One.

FREEWILL CHOICE is a primary gift of God to each of its personalized beings.

The next challenge to Waneka (the Messiah) was a series of battles of the mortal will versus the Spiritual Will, the temptations. These are the temptations of the soul plus the weaknesses of the flesh. The Wavoka (Christ) and the Waneka played out the problems, the heartaches, the questions, and the confusions that beset any spiritual teachers or leaders on Earth. He was presented with a choice and was never forced to play the role of Spiritual Teacher and Messiah.

He freely chose the opportunities presented to him.

As I continue to write this, I feel embraced again by the energy that lifts me all to a higher place. A gentle yet profound and persistent energetic nudging intensifies with each moment of Now.

An essential part of spiritual development is not just accessing higher frequencies of consciousness but understanding how the spiritual and soul realms work. Once you better understand how the soul works, you will be able to consciously work with your soul and easily manifest your potential. When the healing light of love, compassion, and acceptance is shined on the old patterns and fears, they lose their power and are easier to release. Once you let go of old habits of thought and feeling, you become free to turn your attention away from the past and focus on creating the future you would like for yourself and your world. Remember, for the benefit of all concerned. We are one.

The time is unfolding for those of you awakening on Earth to live increasingly in harmony with the higher realms of beings.

You have been helped by many from other realms, but today only two Angels are left on your planet. God's plan and his design for the Earth and humanity is not for higher beings to do the work for humanity, but for human beings to raise their consciousness and heart resonances.

Most of the people chosen to run governments are lawyers. Why would it be that lawyers govern countries? Lawyers are legalists. Satan was a legalist.

They have a history of all this understanding behind them. That would indicate that everything must go through the legal system.

What has happened is that in many places in the world, governments no longer represent the collective heart of humanity. The world has turned into a capitalistic system and, therefore, money speaks louder than the collective.

That is in the process of changing. The changes could probably result in a complete collapse of the system. Then it will be rebuilt on solid ground, which would not be a bad thing. Just get on with it!

The earlier method is currently underway. Capitalism was the most important piece and has been brought into the government. In truth, those that speak the loudest tend to get elected. But we are about to see how loud people can speak. Voices can be heard in different ways. Right now, the political sphere is a circus and represents the frustration that is still not being addressed.

Most do not quite understand what is taking place. These changes are happening in many different areas simultaneously.

It is the collective heart of humanity that will run and rule. Many governments do not represent the collective heart of humanity right now. The love of money is the root of all evil.

We can see what you build from the other side. Dare to dream and let the collective voice be heard.

Your vagus nerve is starting to evolve, so you can feel that compassion even more throughout all humans. This is part of the light-body return that humans are now experiencing. Step forward and stand up. Deal with the best possible and do not wait for the perfect opportunity.

It is here now. So much is taking place. The collective vibration now decides. It means that if you choose to be quiet, you give up your power.

It is time to speak. It is time to claim your willingness and wisdom. Note that it is always perfect, but unless it is offered up there is no possibility of reaching harmony.

Chapter 54
"Ask and you shall receive"

As I, VIE, was once here at great value when Aries became Pisces, now I am here when Pisces is becoming Aquarius. I work now with transforming energy and bringing knowledge to the masses of people.

It all makes sense now; it is all very clear. As we received freedom at birth if you do not ask you will not receive any help. The Bible says it very clearly:

"Ask and you shall receive."

Through ingestion of psychotropic drugs, they put him into a hypnotic trance, disabling his brain's ability to filter information and perception, blocking signals to his conscious mind, and making him act the way that serves them.

But they did not expect me to be knowledgeable enough and to have the ability to contact the other side of the veil.

Yes! I found out that CHADD was still chipped in various places in his body. I also understood that not only the psychotropic drugs but also the dark forces, the black corrupt government in power, have kept him for years not only delusional but also in hallucination. Using drugs and chips and withdrawal to make sure that they could keep controlled. The same way they activated the chip to have him paint the car pink inside... and be able to declare him incompetent in court.

Later on, as CHADD was found competent, funnily enough by the same doctor that declared him incompetent, they tried to use it against him another way. They arrested him for a minor felony, a lie, trying to get him into psychotropic drugs again. They wanted to prove that he needed the drug.

They kept Baker Acting him to send him to behavioral hospitals and drugged him to such an extent that he had two heart attacks. They tried just about everything to eliminate him. They used the entire corrupted system and the psychiatric thuggees. The same ones that were exterminated by an English lord and have rematerialized and infiltrated the country.

They even sent a black man and a white woman to beat him in his room and break his back and tailbone.

I found him, in the morning, lying down on the concrete floor, on his back in the shower. The water was running, and he was unable to move and was in great pain.

I swung my powerful VAJRA, given to me by the Tibetan Monk Salaminian, used the Light language, toned, and used hand signs, and I entered in contact with the Spiritual Court of Heaven asking "The Judge" to take over, which was granted.

A team of spiritual doctors responded and took over and began to work on CHADD's health immediately.

The Russian Priest Orthodox, Father Vladimir Baranski, heard and took care of the archon that had been bothering CHADD since he was born. We will call her here the surrogate mother.

I asked for an immediate activation of the Violet flame.

A beautiful, Black-skinned woman named Abby appeared. She had a goat next to her. "The Scape Goat" – another form of the lamb of God. The lamb of God pushes evil and negativity out. She also removes fears. Abby absorbs all evil and raises it to God.

Pierre Montour de la Roue, who was my distant ancestor, took care of the protective shield all around CHADD. He is a very powerful man with a very powerful chevron.

Then I smelled the scent of lilies and saw two of them opening slowly. Four bodyguards appeared to protect CHADD and me in the next twenty-four hours.

Chapter 55
The Saga Continues

I opened the door to say hello and I heard him calling for help. He was lying down in the bathroom with his tailbone broken. One tall black man and one Caucasian woman entered his room in the middle of the night, dressed in black, beat him in the shower, and left him lying on the floor for hours. One of them commented to the other as they left the room, "I think that we killed him."

The firefighters came, and they rushed him to a hospital where he had surgery. He was released with a deep open wound.

He was released a few days later and given an Asian nurse to take care of his wound each day. One week passed. The Asian nurse came with a "nurse in training" as she called her, and she told me to look carefully at how she was taking care of his wound and to learn from her because I would have to do it from now on. She came one last time with the "nurse in training" who looked much more military than a farmer raising horses as she was pretending to be.

The Sergeant nurse in training (undercover) was looking by the window, talking to someone on her phone and giving the address. Not ten minutes passed, and paramedics arrived and took CHADD to a hospital "for high blood pressure."

I asked one of the paramedics what was the situation with CHADD's blood pressure, and he said, "I have seen worse."

I went to visit CHADD the following day and to my surprise, he was bound to his bed. I called the nurse to ask what was that all about, and she could not answer my question. She could not understand why he was admitted for high blood pressure and was treated that way. She found out later that he had been Baker Acted by the Asian nurse under the pressure of the military sergeant "nurse in training."

She was in fact from the military.

The military lawyer Laryson acted on behalf of Richard Scotty.

This being clarified, I left a few hours later. This was on Christmas Eve. Christmas Day came, and CHADD had mysteriously disappeared from the hospital. Vanished in the middle of the night. Three days later I received a phone call from him. He'd been taken in the middle of the night by Katherine (the surrogate) transported to her new town and admitted to a psychiatric unit to celebrate Christmas. Days passed and I received a phone call from the doctor, who said, "CHADD gave me your phone number. He is now under a psychiatric doctor's care and the hospital is trying to find a state hospital in this town to move him into, but there are none available because of his wound that needs attention."

And he rapidly added, "I have seen his file. His family is pathetic. Treating him this way." CHADD was released with this comment, suffering anguish due to the mistreatment of his family. Pathetic! There is nothing else wrong with him.

As a Christmas present, CHADD received from his family three stamps. One to keep him limited, powerless, and handicapped. Another one is for Katherine to have a pipeline of control and to be able to do anything to him. A third stamp to affect his mind and make him delusional.

My friend, the past Archbishop Fulton Sheen, quickly took action to purify these stamps; then they were burned in a spiritual fire by the violet of transformation by the beautiful Abby.

One week later, Katherine (his father's second wife) called me saying here we are at the library not far from you. Come pick him up and take care of him. He does not have any car or money. I cannot take care of him.

I was taken by surprise and did not know where I could rent him a place to stay but finally found a place.

After a week at the long-stay place, he received a phone call from the manager telling him that he needed to pack and leave. The Thuggees just bought the place.

Then he moved to another similar type of place. Two weeks passed by and I found it funny that the place had changed its name. I researched and discovered that the Thuggees now owned it.

We left for the day, drove out of town for business purposes, and came back in the late afternoon. The room door was opened and breached. Someone had trespassed, and CHADD's personal belongings had been searched. Who was it and for what purpose?

The answer came relatively quickly. The thuggees had bought the place!

About fifteen minutes later someone knocked at the door.

"Who is it?" CHADD asked.

"County Sheriffs. Open the door, please."

CHADD's phone call to the rich old Navy man to finally tell him of his hard life and the maltreatment from Katherine over all the years did not please everybody.

Judge Forrest (dark energy, and military judge, friend of Richard Scotty) was sending the sheriffs to arrest him with the most ridiculous complaint.

"CHADD du Messie, you are arrested for falling and lying on the floor in the parking lot, for listening to TV a little bit too loud, for burning candles to Our Lady of Guadalupe and other saints by the window while reading the Bible and praying and also being in your underwear in your room."

The small female sheriff transported him to jail and put him in solitary confinement. Five days later I found out that it was already prearranged. They were making a claim, saying that CHADD was a danger to himself.

It was a set-up and a conspiracy with the blond manager, the tall black man who was sent there as an observer and asked to make a false statement against him based on what happened, as well as the civilian Spanish-Asian woman who came with the sheriff sent by the judge to arrest him, thanks to his family doctor that contacted his surrogate mother.

It appears that the civilian woman looking like a Spanish-Asian was a humanoid clone sent there to telepathically give orders to the Sheriff from the court to arrest CHADD.

We knew too much about the place. We had uncovered everything. We knew about the drug traffic taking place in the location and about the young teenage girls picked up in front of colleges and sent in rented rooms, forced into prostitution.

We had both received visions of murders, drugs, human trafficking, child prostitution, and porn in the establishments.

They had installed nano cameras in CHADD's room and were listening to our conversations, waiting to make their move.

The arrest of the Latin woman with a baby at the church was an arrest for drug trafficking and was one too many arrests of their drug dealer. They felt it like a threat.

That time I received even more help. The Spirit Historian, Tensing Tao Lo, a Tibetan monk, came to support us. He can read the akashic records of people and can read the akasha of counties and cities as well. He told me how they teach Tibetan monks that life changes and is not static. Knowledge and remembering were going to move us forward.

The forces of evil have worked with all their might to stop CHADD and me and our work. They have worked on my body, mind, and spirit to weaken me, but I have still been moving forward.

I now have a white Roman toga around my body and a clip with diamonds in my hair. My name is Theresa. I am the wife of a powerful Senator, CHADD.

I have been reintroduced to my parents in a previous life. Saint Anne and Saint Joachim. They are not in the physical body but in the spirit. They are now coming to me. They have been blocked by the dark forces, but the dark forces can't control me anymore.

This was not all. I sent a decree to my Star family. My decree was heard, and a council was immediately taken. I am told that it is being discussed and care is being taken in every facet. I will hear it from them directly; they are working with an entire plan to help.

Seven warriors of female vibration with great power came immediately upon my request. They can achieve what even men can't.

Chapter 56
Another Dream

I am far, far away in a profound sleep. I find myself being transported off the planet. Suddenly I am in a spaceship. We are flying fast at a very low altitude between two mountains. There is barely more than an inch left on either side.

Then we reach a higher altitude, but we have to fly between branches and leaves. I think of the deadly damage birds can do to an airplane. But we make it. It's only him and me. I do not see his face – the pilot's face. After what it seems to be a long time of flying at a very low altitude, in a very narrow space, we finally stabilize in a new dimension.

The right door opens to a portal." He" – the pilot – exits through it. He slowly puts his feet out the door, one, then the second foot. I am observing and grabbing it all. It seems that he is walking in the air, kind of like Jesus did on the water. He walks away. I carefully decide to get out by the same door, putting one hesitant foot down. There is no solid ground. My foot is passing through whatever it was that the man could walk on.

I look at the opposite side, and there is another door. I walk towards the other door, which is open. On my way towards it, I see a very fast projection of sacred geometric symbols that pass rapidly outside of the open door, from left to right. I keep walking towards the door, pass through the door to exit, and I find myself merging into the higher realm setting. This grants me a higher authority for transformation with groups or individuals that can bring profound change. I understand the extent of my mission here with him.

I am now able to simply lift off old sabotaging patterns that kept us restricted and limited in the experience of our lives.

I see that Karma is no longer in operation, affecting health and preventing us from claiming and receiving our natural abundance.

As the observer, I became the witness of the challenge.

Christ must burn first of all in our human body. Later, the flame must take place in the depths of the soul. And, finally, at the bottom of the spirit. These three steps through the seven spheres are profoundly significant. These three basic steps are contained in the seven spheres of the world and the Universe. Easter is deeply significant, and has very deep esoteric roots, because the initiate must work on the lunar forces, and the forces of Mercury, Venus, the Sun, Mars, Jupiter, and Saturn. The Logos operates in seven regions and according to the seven planets of the solar system.

Your Divine inner consciousness is an active light within your being that vibrates at the same frequency as the Creator and, therefore, holds the true and pure consciousness of the Creator. Your Divine inner consciousness simply exists within you. When you engage with it, the results are states of Love, Harmony, Peace, Unity, and acceptance. These states fill every cell of your being and every aspect of your etheric (auric) field, feelings, and thoughts.

Pain is born from the judgment of separation. When any judgment arises within, acknowledge it first, then let it go by breathing it away in a white bubble of Light.

The electromagnetic fields of the heart and brain are reflections of emotional states that get the body into frequencies that alter biological expression. We need self-conscious observation. Mechanical self-observation never leads to anything.

Aging should not exist. It has been implanted in our minds, like the idea of physical death.

I was returned in a completely transformed state.

Nothing was familiar. This was a new beginning.

Chapter 57
Understanding the Parasitic Nature of "Things"

Judas said, "Behold, the authorities (Archons) dwell above us, so it is they who will rule over us."

Archons or Psycho-Spiritual Parasites are weird species made of organic (silicon-based) elements.

The Savior said, "It is you who will rule over them. But only when you rid yourselves of jealousy, and take on the protection of the Light, and enter the nymphion (bridal chamber)."

The Savior-teacher is emphatic that we have power over the Archons, but he also makes it clear that some human failings impede the use of our power.

Although they cannot access our genetic structure, they may affect or distort our sense of our genetic makeup. The Anunnaki are a highly advanced non-human species that inhabit the planet Niburu.

There are two types of Archons identified: a neonate or embryonic type (the big-headed, big-eyed Greys), and a draconic or reptilian type. They present an identical match to the two kinds of ETs most frequently reported in modern times, the Greys, and the Reptilians.

These entities envy all of our Divine aspects and creative abilities because they don't possess any themselves. They feed on our fear. These critters create the veil; they create the shadow of the ego, emotional pain, the body, and all diseases, and fixed belief systems of lack and fear.

They became angry for this reason, and because they can't be like us, they have developed their agenda, getting humanity to be like them, which so far, they have excelled at. They have done an excellent job in getting humans to be like them, through the use of covert mind control.

Through the idea of using electromagnetic shielding, the military, according to conspiracy theorists, wanted to know its potential for psy-wars, psychological warfare meant to destroy the enemy by inducing psychosis and even schizophrenia. They knew of the powerful effects of EM waves on the human brain and body, but they went far beyond, using it on civilians. The military has successfully developed a means of time travel and teleportation, trapping people and then returning them home with plenty of mental illnesses.

They are energy beings. They are created only from energy, without consciousness or soul. They do not possess any Divine aspects. They are negative energy loops that cause us to repeat mistakes in a fractal way. They get their energy from pain, fear, and negative emotions. They exist in the astral realm, which is both inside and outside of us. They or the negative emotions and situations they create are the cause of all diseases. The main way they affect our DNA is through miasms. They pollute the DNA, distort the life force, and pollute the energies of the body. These miasms affect our body and our thinking. Everyone is born with at least one of these miasms.

Archons are the most immediate and intimate threat to humanity.

The main danger we face from them is what they can do, not what humans falsely believe they can do. Their delight is bitter, and their beauty is depraved. Their pleasure is in deception, and deception is from the devil. The Archons can affect your mind by subliminal conditioning techniques. Their main tactics are mental error, intellectual virus, false ideology, especially religious doctrines, and simulation.

The magical journey of awareness in which all involved with Gaia's dreaming is deviated from or distorted by an alien influence." Human beings are on a journey of awareness, which has been momentarily interrupted by extraneous forces."

Though a special link to the Goddess, our species can overcome the Archons and secure a human and humane future for the Earth by using the weapons of Love to combat evil.

Even though Lyn (from the public defender's office) keeps visiting CHADD in confinement to tell him that it's going to be okay, and they do not understand why he has been arrested, three weeks later he is sitting in jail.

For CHADD, it became clear that the corrupted Military Judge Forrest, from the dark government, was repeating what he did before and did not record. Double jeopardy in an asylum's admission is becoming triple jeopardy.

His family doctor, Dr. Vasdgy, gave me, VIE, a copy of his last visit in a file one month ago at CHADD's request. The progress note was clear: "CHADD is not under any medication." I mailed it to the public defender's office and other people involved in his defense.

Two months passed, then I finally received a phone call from CHADD.

"They have moved me to Hope & Dream Healthcare Snakinville. I am very tired and there is no bed to sleep in. The place is overbooked, and it is not handicap accessible. I can't take a shower and using the bathroom is a dangerous adventure."

He was immediately injected with three shots and fell asleep on his chair.

My mind is a mishmash of dreams and reality.

CHADD woke up and went to look for a phone and called me again. By the tone of his voice, I knew that they had shot him with some psychotropic drugs. I picked up on the unbalance of the vibration and the tone of his voice.

Eighteen days later CHADD has a "review." Not less than 12 doctors are in the meeting. They look at him with their fixed, angry eyes. I can feel the emptiness and see the lack of soul. They discuss his case with hate. Then the Indian doctor finally said that he was going to prescribe him a psychotropic drug, Adderall, that CHADD refused.

The following day CHADD was awoken by the nurse telling him that he was going to be transported to court.

He was pushed in his wheelchair outside the building into a room that was "the court."

The same judge and the same doctors as before were part of the farce. They discussed his case in front of him and ignored him. They were rude. The Asian doctor, whom he saw for the first time in nineteen days, had no problem whatsoever lying to the judge. He told the judge that CHADD should not be released and had thrown his food at his face. They sentenced him to eight more weeks before another review and transported him back to jail in confinement.

The reality is that CHADD is among over 700 people who are kept in jail under psychotropic drugs. The offenses that put them in jail are minor: loitering, disturbing the peace, public intoxication. Inmates are awakened each day and given psychotropic drugs. "Schizophrenia" has become the Ebola of behavioral disorders," the Orlando Sentinel reported. The judicial system, the Archons in place, determines when "the mentally ill" inmate is released.

The Thuggee psychiatrist's archons have ensured that "more and more people are being deceived into thinking that the best answer to life's many routine problems and challenge lies with the 'latest and greatest' psychiatric drugs," according to the Citizens Commission on Human Rights.

Hundreds of news outlets reported that 'The war on drugs' has taken on a literal twist, with ISIS fighters being fueled by a stimulant drug known as Captagon, a pharmaceutical cousin of the ADHD drug, Adderall.

"The drugs quickly produce a euphoric intensity in users, allowing fighters to stay up for days, killing with a numb, reckless abandon," wrote the Washington Post. Captagon is a 'toxic fuel' that creates 'super-human' fighters."

In November, an article, "Breaking Bad: the Stimulant Drug that Links Isis and the Nazis," was posted on the world's leading English language website for news analysis of the Middle East, pointing out, "ISIS is far from the first murderous group to drug its fighters before battle..."

Psychiatry has hooked our world on drugs. A public service report from the Citizen Commission on Human Rights says that while posing as authorities on the mind and mental health, psychiatry has no scientific basis for any treatments or methods.... Psychiatric disorders are not medical diseases... Psychiatrists claim that brain scans now show brain changes that 'prove' mental disorders, such as schizophrenia and depression, are brain-based. There is no scientific evidence to prove this...Psychotropic drugs are increasingly being exposed as chemical toxins with the power to kill."

The Anunnaki Greys and Reptilians are the negative energy in our Government that hooks our world on drugs.

Chapter 58
Time to Move Forward

The work has been done.

This was the end of the fight. There is confirmation. The center of the Earth now turned blue first and a few weeks later rose sunset.

The time of acceptance is for beings to let go and let God. To let go and to open to all imperfections of who beings are at this moment within humanness.

Cracks are appearing through the veils. Now is the time to move forward. The frequency of the reflecting light of the sun will enhance the ability to align with the energy of the framework supporting the transition through multi-dimensional settings.

To assist you in actualizing your higher purpose and your greatest calling in this embodiment, you are invited to exercise your mastery by choosing to bring God's Love and Light into all your thoughts, senses, and actions. Your body, your mind, and your spirit restore God's loving consciousness.

You are encouraged to shine your heart space from the Divine Omniscient and dare to be who you are.

Stand in your heart space and stay balanced through the great love coming from Heaven's realm, straight to your illuminated heart chamber, which links you directly with us.

Follow the path of Oneness and Divine love and remember that Christ brought the instrument of ultimate creativity that could transmute human violence: "The Eucharist," or True Christ.

The Creator is now totally in charge. The battle is finished, and we have won. But they still do not know it.

Paul sent his neighbor Dave to beat him up. Dave was part of the conspiracy to ransom CHADD. As CHADD did not have any money then, Dave beat him up. The very first time CHADD was severely hurt on the head again. That happened only a few days after he was admitted.

As time passed, Dave made a second attempt to collect some money. That time CHADD was hurt in the chest. It looks like a repetition of Carlos beating him. One rib was broken.

CHADD was driven out of the place, fifty miles away to have some x-rays. The doctors saw that the broken bone was very close to the heart and that CHADD's life was in danger. But he was still driven back to his cold and humid concrete cell that the state has the nerve to call a room.

About a month later, CHADD was moved to another part of the building. There, Carlos (father) was waiting for him on camera. Of course, they need to make money on everything he does. His reactions, his conversation, his behavior…

Then VIE received a phone call from Danny, one of the trapped people there who was helping and protecting CHADD while he was in this violent location.

Danny: VIE, I know that you never did that to him, but you must listen to what I have to tell you. His father's wife had the Court send him an official document on your behalf that restrained CHADD from talking to you. It's saying that you asked for this because CHADD was harassing you with phone calls. I have seen the document, and though it's not from you, it's an official document. I learned the details from my guides. It is this woman that he calls "my earthy father's wife, the surrogate." I think that her name is Katherine. She asked the court to send this restraining order from "you" to him to separate both of you for money purposes. But also, because she wants to manipulate him better while he is on psychotropic drugs. She is all about money and never has enough."

To separate to better reign over and control him. VIE: I never thought that the dark government, the Black Court, would go so far. But it reminds me that three weeks earlier I had a message left on my phone telling me that in September of the previous year, the court ordered that I stop talking to him or any other person in the state location where he was sent.

Of course, I immediately called my lawyer who found nothing like it at all, and not even a case number for CHADD's charges or why he was maintained in a state location.

Chapter 59
The Awakening of the Dove

Some beings were called to travel to various locations for the awakening of the Dove and to anchor the different parts of the Dove.

They anchored the Dove with stones from other places.

The Yucatan is the last part to be anchored. To anchor the heart, a group of ten met in Arkansas to open the imprint patterning of the heart. All ten were called from other places and didn't know each other. They found a very strong energy in place with the awakening and opening coming from the first and the second portal, forming a pyramid. They noted the presence of Jesus and Mary, among many others.

The energy held by the framework is designed to move the heart beyond illusion and align it with the state of self-acceptance.

It attracted the attention of the authorities in charge of the movie they were making about CHADD and VIE without their consent. They decided that it was urgent to finish it.

This is why they arrested CHADD immediately and sent him away from VIE.

Chapter 60
Visions are Now Explained

I had another vision. It was the same vision two days in a row. My purse was stolen, but I still had my wallet.

This is the explanation I was given by my spiritual guides.

Then another king will appear; he will be very different from the earlier ones and will overthrow three kings... He will try to change their religious laws...

Then the heavenly court will sit in judgment, take away his power, and destroy him completely. The power and greatness of all the kingdoms on earth will be given to the people of the Supreme God.

I saw one man coming to me who would try to get me on his side, thinking that he could steal my work, gifts, and power for his profit and become very well-known around the world. Thinking that he will be able to receive 10 percent from all the churches. Wanting to trap human beings, with my help and consent, in the third dimension by founding a new church under the name of "The Last Conveyer" that he would build all over the world based on the Old Testament only.

But the time has come, and humans are ready to move forward, beyond all the facets of a third-dimensional consciousness.

The Old Testament is a book of rules and regulations and was necessary for the time when unevolved society needed rules. But two thousand years ago, an enlightened teacher proclaimed that he came to bring a New Testament. This New Testament was meant to supersede the old, guiding mankind into consciousness based on Love and Oneness. However, to this day, many still hold to the rules of the Old Testament while calling themselves Christians.

Human beings are moving into the New Testament state of consciousness, where the self as well as all living things are honored and respected as being in and of the Divine.

Resistance could make something unimportant into a powerful enemy that needs to be eliminated or overcome. Through Karma, through previous lives, unwanted habits, and qualities flow from cellular memory, from the previous lifetimes when they were necessary for survival. Human beings must stop struggling and put forward their intention to spiritually evolve. They should not forget that they have spiritual guides.

They must not buy into the fear energy, because fears are presented to them by parasites' energy, the system in power, the government, experts, most churches...

Unfortunately, many are forced into psychotropic drugs, and it gets them into cloudiness of mind fear, and unwanted thoughts.

This is what we call acts of terrorism or fanaticism. Unfortunately, most become their puppets and are driven into these acts of violence.

VIE: I looked out the window and the eagle was staring up at me, on the fence.

I stared back at him for a few seconds, then he flew right towards me and perched at the corner of the roof very close, stared at me again, went back on the fence then flew away.

The message was delivered. He confirmed to me: "Twice they stole your purse, and twice you saw that you still had your wallet. They could not take it from you."

Now Pierre, my ancestor, is with me, and this is what he says.

"When people dream of a mouth, it means that it is how you integrate things, and when you dream of eyes it is your I."

Archangel Gabriel made his presence and assistance known this morning.

I had a little private time with him then. Here is what I want to tell you now.

Health carries karma from previous lives. Things are carried over. Stubbornness and fear can lock up your body. Fears are carried over, lifetime to lifetime. Humans came to Earth to experience Love.

Jupiter this year until August will allow you to heal in a manner that has nothing to do with medicine. Karma does not lock in inability, but the dark forces that control the planet want to prevent human beings from achieving independence and restrain them from becoming their own master. There is a big movement to keep people sick.

The reliable people are Aquarius, Scorpio, Leo, and Taurus.

The actual President is manipulated. He cannot do much because of his pride.

Chapter 61
Genetically Modified DNA

This planet is populated by energy parasites.

Chief Anu had two sons. Let's say Satan and Lucifer. One legitimate, and the other one not. One, Enlil, runs things from space. He founded Jehovah's command of the air. The second is Enki, and he is still alive. The interstellar colony is from Niburu. Part of Enki's empire destroyed Atlantis with the change of weather. He has various facilities all over the world.

Time is an illusion that structures people. It holds places. The Anunnaki, whose time sequences it is on, have made time on Earth.

No one today can be unaware of the complex global problems of environmental degradation, species extension, toxic chemical soil depletion, and deforestation. Global warming and desertification.

Enki has been the first Anunnaki to hazard a trip to Earth to begin a mining operation for gold.

Enlil now controls the Anunnaki royal succession.

The connection between humans and Anunnaki is much more profound than that of masters and slaves. All evidence strongly suggests the DNA of Anunnaki was mixed with that of humans. This was because the Anunnaki needed someone to work the mines in search of gold, ORME, and other precious metals.

This is how the Anunnaki took control of humanity. They are patrons and founders. They were teachers and justices, they were technologists and kingmakers, but even venerated as archons and masters, they were not idols or worshiped as the ritualistic gods of subsequent cultures were.

The word that was eventually translated as "worship" was "avod."

The Anunnaki presence may baffle historians. Their language is confusing to linguists, and their advanced techniques may perplex scientists but to dismiss them would be foolish.

The Anunnaki were the council of Gods and Goddesses and periodically met to consider their future actions concerning each other.

The Anunnaki are the Nephilim, the fallen Angels (according to the book of Joshua). Anunnaki has been also equated with the "watchers" from the books of Daniel and Jubilees.

All you have been told is a lie. Just about everything you have been taught is a lie.

Hopi and Apache lineage ties together the missing pieces that schools and churches do not want you to know.

This is indeed a slave planet where you have been genetically modified (DNA) to become subservient slaves.

The reliable people are Aquarius, Scorpio, Leo, and Taurus.

The NWO does not have a government, but they have put a system in place through corporations.

They are attempting to put it in place also with the U.N.

Their thought, what they are trying to implant, is that one religion will be easier to control than one world currency.

They call Wi-Fi the "we fry you people." RTintel is what your mobile is. They study you, what you do, and your habits and patterns. There will come a time when people tear down all the towers and the electronics that are destroying the world. When you are in electronics, your brain goes "bye-bye."

There are still solutions, though.

Stay grounded. Connect to Earth this time.

Put your aura in three layers. Gold, the rose sunset, blue or green. Put the cloak over. Be invisible and unnoticed. This is the end of the games.

People are going to wake up angry. They will not be able to think logically or reason. And this is what has been pushing people into emotional crisis.

This is what is immediate today.

The power of the mind to boost the immune system is to say over and over, "I am going to be fine."

Repeat like a mantra to change the frequency, "I am in joy, I am in joy..." then send it to the Earth.

They want to stop the change you can make, and this is what has been brought about by Harry Potter, for the most part.

We are in a massive change. We are close to the end, yet people are in an emotional crisis with no logic.

Atlanteans are back on Earth using their grigri, manipulating, and controlling human beings. The founder of Atlantis was in charge of crystals on Earth ...and he has laboratories.

But while most of the controlling extraterrestrials on this planet are malevolent, you have received help from benevolent Pleiadians, who are trying to help undo what the Reptilians, Sirians, and malevolent Anunnaki have set up on this planet for you.

In August 1947, six Apache Indians on a vision quest, including Sky's grandfather, rescued the lone surviving Pleiadian, called a Star Elder. This particular Pleiadian used crystals to project images to communicate the history of the solar system and mankind itself.

According to Morning Sky, the light at the end of the tunnel leads to a soul regeneration center where your soul becomes trapped in the reincarnation cycle on this planet, to get people to continue serving these entities in place. The Reptilians were given free rein on the planet to have people go into the tunnel of light. Still, according to Morning Sky, the Sirians are responsible for all religions/cults, to control man.

EAU was changed to YAHWEH=Jehovah DA EA DEUS=GOD

(EA-SU=Jesus) EASU planted clues deep within caves and caverns all around the planet to help you remember who you are and how to get out of the system in place.

(ESAU=the works of) Some of the ESAU are responsible for building the pyramids and the face on Mars.

Marduk, MAR (MR-son of) DUK (dog Sirius).

Marduk was identified with the planet Mars.

The system said don't let them know, because a little over fifty percent of them would stand up and say, "I want these aliens out, I want the Greys out...We are going to take over and we have the right to do it and we are going to make this planet a free-willed, passionate and all loving empire," and the system does not want that.

The current administrators of the empire government on the planet have lineage back to ORION hybrid Reptilians, while the money was given to Marduk's children, the Rockefellers, and the Rothschilds. Rockefeller (RA-KA Pharaohs) and the Rothschild.

(RA-KA-M-RE KAM) (KAM=shield=Rothschild)

Rockefellers and Rothschilds are both part of this war consciousness.

Morning Sky also said," There is a war, and we are the prize."

Chapter 62
Arcturus

Arcturus is one of the most advanced civilizations in this galaxy. It is a fifth-dimensional civilization and a prototype of Earth's future.

Its energy works as an emotional, mental, and spiritual healer for humanity and also a gateway through which humans pass during death and rebirth. It is the mid-way programming center used by the physical brotherhoods in this universe to govern many rounds of experience with pyramids at the end of the galaxy.

The Arcturians work in close connection with the ascended Master when they call the brotherhoods of all. They also work closely with the Galactic command.

They teach that the most fundamental ingredient for living in the fifth dimension is Love. Negativity, fear, and guilt must be overcome and exchanged for Love and Light.

The Arcturians have been working with Earth since life first started on this planet. They have many bases on Earth, and they have three bases on the moon. Many of their bases on Earth are inside mountains.

They are here to assist humans in centering the fourth and fifth dimensions of reality and in raising their vibrational frequencies. They stand as the guardians and protectors of humanity but have had a difficult time dealing with the government and the military, who are primarily interested in military technology, not spiritual enlightenment.

The Arcturians could help in even greater and more open capacities than man, but the people who govern the U.S. and the world are so materialistically and egoistically oriented that they resist the help of these incredibly advanced beings.

Why does the government not want to officially admit to the existence of UFOs?

Instead, the U.S. government made a deal with the Greys, who are very selfish beings interested in taking over the world for their greedy purposes. ETs want a one-world government. They selected electronics and brought them to this planet for that reason.

Anunnaki have been fooling around and one-third of the population of the world lives on two dollars a day.

Chapter 63
Lanterns on the Water

I had the vision of Lotus lanterns floating from the horizon line to the shore. In each lantern was a glowing white light. The water was blue, still, and clear. Mary appeared at the far horizon and moved towards me, floating above the water. She reached me and entered me.

I received a phone call from a stranger.

His voice was panicked. "Are you VIE?"

"Yes!"

"Listen, VIE, please tell me that I have not gone crazy. The trees are talking to me now since you raised my energy. What is happening to me?"

During the convention, a young woman approached me and asked me if I could help her, saying that she could not have any children. I tried to get in a corner next to the entrance of a private salon, and I laid my hands upon her and began to pray. But the words sprayed quickly and the surroundings and lines behind grew bigger and bigger. The love, peace, and joy reflected on her face were attracting the crowd. Suddenly she opened her eyes and said: "My God, what is happening to me? It's wonderful. I can even clearly hear the radio now, and I feel so different."

The vision became clear to me. In healing the suffering, we free them from fear, anguish, and the dark, and we guide them to liberation quicker, to the return to the law of One, unity with animals and plants. To heal suffering is a much bigger word than we give to it. All that employ themselves to relieve the suffering of animals are working for urgent and necessary liberation.

The dark entities are also killing animals and plants. Dogs, sharks, dolphins, horses, bees... Water is polluted, and without water, we can't live.

Animals depend on us. The chemicals in pest control are killing the bees and destroying and polluting the land. Trees are dying...

Animals carry a soul and the law of One is to always work together, and not to divide ourselves due to our divergence of sensibility.

All the illness of humanity comes from fear, anxiety, and anguish, and there is a method to it.

Praying is the only solution and the way to re-coordinate body, soul, and spirit. The cause of illness is the lack of harmony between the personality and the soul. Human beings must become conscious of the divinity in themselves and in consequence, its power over illness. Fear does not have a place in man.

Early Christian, Essenian, Druid, and Egyptian priests all practiced the laying on of hands and praying.

Religions are temporary locales, adaptations of the law of One, the religion of One God. It is coming back with the Aquarius era. All religions have been taught by the Cosmic Christ during one of his reincarnations as Jesus Christ. It is him, this Christian conscience, that we address when we are praying. There is only One law in the big religions of the world: God is unique, He is One.

"You will love him with all your strength and your Soul, and you will love your brother like yourself."

Jesus became Christ by aligning his frequency to the frequency of the Father. And it was only as Jesus Christ, in His last incarnation, that he terminated totally what he had created as Adam (with Eve, his soul sister, reincarnated in Mary).

This is why we owe allegiance to the image of Christ to retrieve our lost divinity and use it to find our divine power.

We recover health by connecting to the Cosmic Christ and through him our creative forces.

Our three bodies (physical, mental, and spiritual) stay connected by the activity of our major glands.

Pituitary, pineal, thyroid, thymus, adrenals, gonads, and Lyden's cell. These glands produce hormones that play an important role. Each organ depends on one of these centers.

Every disease occurs through a dysfunction of one of these centers.

All cures occur by the cleaning of each gland. Specific sound frequencies open these glands that then get into a trance and reach the elevation of the vibrations. This vibratory state allows healing through prayers and meditative prayers. The opening of these centers must be done by someone carrying the vibratory transformational healing energy to avoid the danger of manipulation by a dark entity. Or you'll be a prisoner of an entity.

Rock concerts, where the music is created to put the listener into a trance, hammer violently and constantly on the gland centers and open them. Raping consciousness by subliminal messages. Rock uses a musical technique, making the chakras open without protection. The listener can't feel himself anymore and becomes prey to an entity.

In the New Testament, Jesus stated that all sins can be forgiven, but he also stated that the one sin that can never be forgotten is to speak against the Holy Spirit.

Sister Faustina had a vision of Hell. Saint Maria Faustina Kowalska of the congregation of our Lord of Mercy was led by an Angel to the chasms of hell. A place of great torture.

"I, Sister Faustina Kowalska, by the order of God, have visited the abysses of Hell so that I might tell souls about it and testify to its existence...the devils were full of hatred for me, but they had to obey me at the command of God. What I have written is but a pale shadow of the things I saw. But I noticed one thing: Most of the souls disbelieved that there is hell." (diary 741)

"Do not let the material things blind you, that they did not become a stumbling block in your existence" was given in the Lord's Prayer to the apostles.

Many here do not recognize the term "Neocon" which means "New World Order Fascist." Most people appear not to notice the similarity between the fascism of Nazi Germany and the conservative Christian movement in America.

The high point of the New World Order strategy was to invade Iraq. That resulted in the murder of many Christians there and the rise of ISIS. Not many people seem to clearly understand what is happening in modern America in the area of religion. The globalist movement is an alliance based on self- self-interest of the private international financiers and the royal dynasties. Their agenda is to bring all of Earth's inhabitants under the control of a single state. It's a dangerous, small, and powerful elite circle, working together to take away all freedom. The globalists have found that the best strategy is to play security and liberty, social consciousness, and scripture against each other. They have created great tension, and the controversies coming from different directions are to their benefit, keeping people arguing with each other. They divide to better reign and to render ineffective people's attempts to unite to learn the truth behind the New World Order agenda.

The Lakota end-of-time prophecy is the prophecy about the black snake that could end the world. It says that from the North a black snake will come. It will cross the sacred land, slowly killing all that it touches, and in its passing, the water will become poisonous. It will endanger all the drinking water from the Missouri River.

The Dakota pipeline can't go through, or only robotic people will exist. There will be no humans, no marine mammals...

Chapter 64
Manulea

One side of my brain insisted that the physically distracting new signals were caused by some important detail that I had missed. Was this, I wondered, the clue? I had two options, but the first seemed more constructive. Having made my choice, I used the quick switch method. At once I felt a signal vibrating in me. I followed it and came upon a scene.

There are many "misguided" Souls. Other Souls do not possess the best intentions or are simply controlled by beings without a body whose intentions are not very commendable and whose evolutionary processes are not commendable.

Unfortunately, these misguided Souls, or the controlled Souls, can be people in important places, where freedom and lives depend on them. Many have abdicated their free will to the will of others by becoming followers and joiners, and they become the effects of other people, becoming the instruments of these souls that do not possess the best intentions. Free will is a gift to everybody from our Creator, but I see that we are living in a war of interest. It's the time when there is a battle between good and evil.

Some Souls were not abducted by free will but fell into the hands of those in power places in the system who took control of their freedom. I have shown that I have good reason to believe that it is what happened to my blue flame. I have written of the consequences to his life.

A deep inner surge immediately gave me answers.

There is a national tragedy of jails and prisons run by corporations. The United States has more people in jail than any other country, including China, an authoritarian country four times our size. And they are all put under psychotropic drugs, for the profit of Big Pharma. Some 2.2 million people are incarcerated.

I slipped in through the front wall and in the foyer, I encountered a woman. She was expecting me. She said, "I am Manuela" She pointed her finger towards a screen, and I read.

The Orlando Sentinel headlined "In Crisis – A Special Report on the Mental Illness." The paper reported that in Florida, jails and prisons have replaced mental hospitals. They are the asylums of the new millennium, according to the Florida Supreme Court. People are not brought here to jail because of mental illness but because they broke a law. Often a minor law—loitering, disturbing the peace, public intoxication. In Florida, jails and prisons have replaced mental hospitals. They are the asylums of the new millennium.

The existence of the private for-profit prison industry, which makes millions from the incarceration of Americans, must end. These private prisons interfere with the administration of justice. And they are driving inmate populations skyward by corrupting the political process.

No one should be allowed to profit from putting more people behind bars, whether inmates in jail or immigrants held in detention centers. The horror stories from for-profit prisons are plentiful. For-profit prisons abuse prisoners, and prisons have merged with mental hospitals, and here are just a few results.

I am seeing rat-infested food served to inmates and other rotten and spoiled food items served to inmates. Inmates are underfed. They are all underweight, lacking nutrients, and subject to viruses, bacteria, and cold. Some are dead from it. I see violent assault. She says privately run prisons reportedly have two to three times the rate of violent assault as publicly run facilities.

The movie continues with projected scenes. A private prison vendor has reportedly used juvenile offenders in Florida to subdue other young prisoners. The children are used by the staff members to inflict harm on other children. The physically disabled are not an exception; they are also sent to jails and prisons, State places for profit, and these State places are not handicapped equipped. There are no bars in the bathrooms or showers. The staff are making jokes and laughing, contemplating inmates falling or not being able to reach the bathroom on time.

Now some nurses in the private prisons have threatened to strike over the inadequate health care. They describe unsafe conditions. There have been reported incidents of patient abuse.

I have witnessed private corporations profiting off detentions have grown to have enormous influence over how and where immigrants are detained. The government is using what is supposed to be Freedom of Information Act exemptions to conceal the behavior of private corporations. The government has redacted substantive portions of the contracts with the private companies, claiming exemptions to protect trade secrets. Sixty-two percent of detention beds are administered by private prison corporations. The redacted information would show what the companies are making per person per day and how tiered pricing works, as well as reveal the guaranteed minimum. Under tiered pricing, the more people the government sends to a location or company, the cheaper it is per person, creating a "perverse incentive" across the system to detain more people and transfer them long distances away from family and counsel.

The IWN (Incarceration Watch Network) co-director Tahnee Peterson talks about the politics of immigration in the age of mass incarceration. "In recent years immigrants have become the fastest-growing population behind bars. Immigration policy has become increasingly linked to the growth of mass incarceration, private prisons, and police border militarization. The greater the share of the detention system operated by private corporations, the less transparent the system gets. These policies have a real human impact on families and individuals caught up in the system. The line between the government and private contractors is thinner than ever. The government has placed the interests of private prison corporations above the interests of the public.

There are assaults and claims of sexual abuse at juvenile prisons in Florida according to a review of state records and accounts from former employees and inmates. Young Services International Executive declined interview requests over several months."

I am hearing a piece of beautiful music now. My left and right brain are suddenly synchronous and unified.

Are you an Angel? You look to me real and normal, Manulea.

Wait! Please wait!

Manulea said, "Look! Your co-worker has been the catalyst of this whole mission and has been deprived of freedom, free will, pride, life, and money and used for profit by the misguided Souls or controlled Souls, with the co-operation of his relatives and friends. His image has been destroyed by many Baker Acts and admission to mental hospitals and jails. Now he is arrested and incarcerated far from his hometown. He has been forced against his will to ingest psychotropic drugs, beaten, and his Achilles tendons cut for no medical reason while in a coma due to an overdose of prescribed drugs. He has been stolen from, poisoned… and presented to your friends, acquaintances, relatives, and the world as mentally incompetent. His brain has been manipulated by high-frequency devices and some people with no souls (clones, some type of humanoid robots) while on psychotropic drugs, and he may be facing years."

Let's stand together and stop this freedom- controllers that destroy everything but also our health for money. We'll see fairness return to our judicial systems. Those who sit in judgment of others, and in important key places in the government and the planet, will be replaced by elders that have been chosen because of their wisdom and compassion.

But what about...

Manulea laughed and said, "Love conquers all!! All is well now VIE. All pieces of the puzzle are fitting into places," and she shrank back and vanished

Chapter 65
Like a Thief in the Middle of the Night

I centered myself so that my energies were as focused as they could be with contemplative or meditative prayer. This calms me down and enables me to connect to the other side of the veil.

Although I had some previous experiences, I was taken by surprise.

A beautiful round mirror appeared in my vision. I looked at the mirror and I saw a monastery and the monk Thomas Merton chanting among the other monks.

Then a sheet of paper reappeared for me to read. Calling To Remembrance the participation in Our

Lord & Agony in Gethsemane of Saint Maria Faustina Kowalska of the Blessed Sacrament, who at least thrice in her lifetime willingly accepted the violent pains that convulsed her for three hours and at times caused her to lose consciousness, as allowed by Jesus to offer reparation to God for infants murdered in their mother's wombs.

To all members of The Eucharistic Apostles of the Divine Mercy (A Lay Ministry Outreach of the Congregation of Marians of the Immaculate Conception of the Most Blessed Virgin Mary) and To all the faithful worldwide, who joined them in offering The Divine Mercy Chaplet

(Revealed to St. Faustina for averting divine chastisement).

For mothers, that they not abort their offspring; For infants in danger of being put to death in the womb; for a change of heart of the providers of abortions and their collaborators; for human victims of stem cell research, genetic manipulation, cloning, and euthanasia; and for all entrusted with the government of people that they may promote the "Culture of Life" to put an end to the "Culture of death."

I impart a Superabundance of Divine Graces,

My Heartfelt Apostolic Blessings. Pope John Paul ll I was now shown the Clock of the Divine Mercy Chapel that indicates that four minutes are left before three PM.

I normally make sure during the week to stop by the church at three pm to participate in the three o'clock praying group, but I never went before on a Sunday. There must be a reason, I thought.

I let my spirit check who was the praying team and I was curious to see if there was one group praying on Sundays.

Two minutes later, after I entered the chapel, I saw a Spanish woman coming towards me. She asked me to lead the Rosary Prayer as she had a sore throat. I accepted and I began the Prayer. Even though there were two men and another woman there, I found myself leading nobody but myself. I was alone saying the prayer aloud. Five minutes into the prayer, the man in the row in front of me turned towards me and weirdly looked at me. I wondered what this was. Then the woman with the sore throat began to read something aloud though I was still praying. I still did not get it.

Then a woman from the Philippines, Chi Linh, spoke, asking me: Is that the Divine Mercy prayer? I was even more confused and lifted my hands in a sign, saying do not ask me.

Suddenly An Ming appeared, a Chinese woman. She knelt behind the last bench, just behind Chi Linh, and began to lead everyone into finishing the Rosary. Then she continued with the Divine prayer, said Amen, and left, followed by Chi Linh. I decided to join them outside.

An Ming asked both of us for our names and our contact information. She said you must join us, the group of women at night. I will text you the dates and hours. All three of us must pray together. Also, next month you must come to the Blessing at Saint Jude.

I discovered later that she was from the group the "Legion of Mary."

We found out that the three of us, Chi Ming, An Linh, and me, VIE, were born in January on the 21st, 22nd, and 23rd, and that we were all three Aquarius.

Then An Ming insisted to Chi Linh and me, "We need to pray, the three of us together with the group of the Legion of Mary women at night each week." She added, "We have to be prepared. Jesus said that he will come back like a thief. It is the time."

I replied, "Yes, he told me like a thief in the middle of the night." (That is what Jesus told me several times.)

Chi Linh began to describe her vision to us. "I saw Jesus. I saw Jesus. He showed himself to me and there was a bright glowing light all around him..." She began to describe what she saw.

Later, after An Ming left, Chi Linh told me, "I was totally confused with those prayers in the chapel. You were praying, and this lady began to read another prayer aloud at the same time, and I called for help and here I was answered. Jesus sent us An Ming. She came and now we are all Aquarius, from all different backgrounds, and as Ah Ming said, there is a reason. We must stay in contact. Just in case, give me your contact too." And she disappeared with the vision.

A Message from Marie-Madeleine to you

I am Marie-Madeleine. I am His wife. I have always been next to him, and I have an important message for you. We are partners in this adventure. Understand that I am the only one he can trust. He loves you, and you make him continue to suffer. He is the one you are seeking, the one you are longing for.

This is the ultimate battle between human governments and God before the judgment time.

We are living the Divine Mercy Year. Christ is coming back. So, let's pray the "Divine Mercy Prayer" given by Jesus to St. Faustina for the end of time.

Praise Him.

Have faith in Christ. Faith is Love and Love is the only Truth.

LOVE is all there is! Stop fighting, drop your anger, stop the division between all of you. Fight with Love and it will all be well.

Stop judging. Embrace each other. Support each other and send Love to each other. Please! Stop Fighting, stop killing.

Is this Book Fact or Fiction?

About the Author

VIE is French-American. In January 1987, VIE experienced a dramatic shift in consciousness resulting in a complete change of lifestyle.

During her first contact experience, VIE's galactic mission and purpose were revealed and gifts from previous interplanetary incarnations were activated. She is a visionary, vibrational transformation, and metaphysical healer. A book author and musician. VIE speaks the language of the Light that she also sings, tones, chants, and hand-signs. She carries the authority to activate your dormant strands of DNA, raise your energy, erase your stuck emotions, and erase your pain & traumas, which she can feel. She is here to guide you to find your purpose and destiny. She can help you find your path and reconnect you to your blueprint.

VIE is the creator of **Bio-Qi Therapy** and founder of the **Institute of Biostimulation™.** She gives sessions one-on-one in her office or Quantum.

The Mission of the Institute is to present an opportunity for the expansion of awareness in the healing arts of Light and Sound frequencies with her Angel co-workers, during sessions but also with their books and Music.

The purpose of the Institute: awakening new frequencies with One's being.

Our Work

CHADD and I have brought healing to many and are opening the world to a new spiritual realm and preparing all of us for the new divine plan. I work the Light while CHADD works the Sound.

"Though we do not worship money, we do respect it as an energy that is necessary to continue our mission, which is to help you grow spiritually. Your donation is a blessing from your heart, and we greatly and thankfully appreciate it. Thank you.

We Love you very much."

For more information and donations go to:

https://instituteoflightandsound.com

https://www.facebook.com/BioInstituteOfLightandSound

https://twitter.com/BioInstituteLS

http://blogster.com/instituteoflightandsound/

www.ingramcontent.com/pod-product-compliance
Lightning Source LLC
Chambersburg PA
CBHW060523130626
46553CB00002B/625